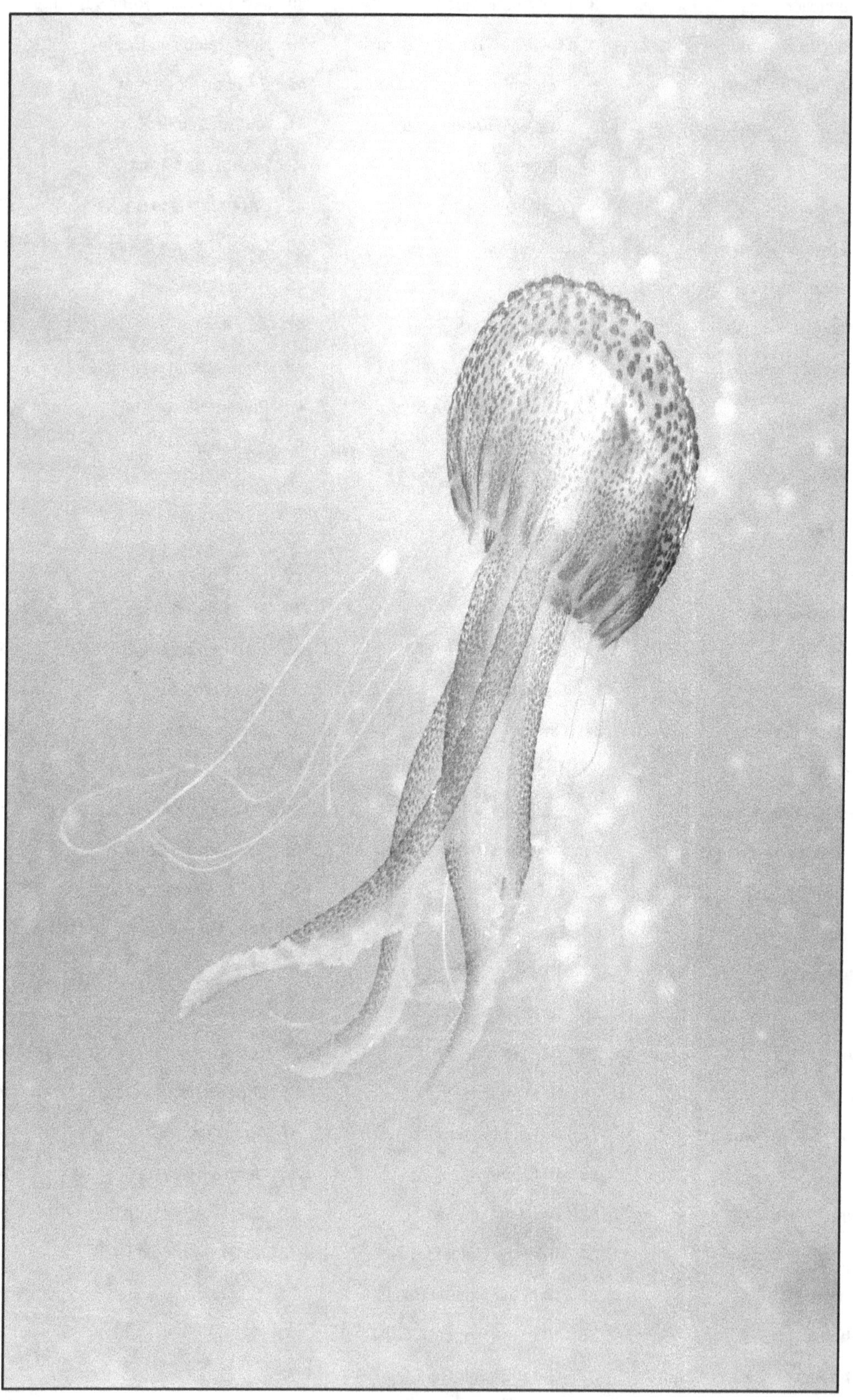

Introduction

Marine life, also known as sea life or ocean life, refers to the plants, animals, and other organisms that live in the salt water of seas or oceans, or the brackish water of coastal estuaries. This includes a wide range of organisms, from the smallest plankton to the largest whale.

Marine life plays a crucial role in our planet's ecosystems. Here are some of its significant contributions:

Regulating Climate: Marine organisms, mostly microorganisms, produce oxygen and sequester carbon.

This process helps regulate the Earth's climate.

Maintaining Biodiversity: The ocean is home to a diverse range of species, contributing to the planet's biodiversity.

As of 2023, more than 242,000 marine species have been documented, and perhaps two million marine species are yet to be documented.

Providing Food and Livelihoods: The ocean provides food and facilitates livelihoods for millions, if not billions, of people.

Shaping and Protecting Shorelines: Marine life, in part, shapes and protects shorelines. Some marine organisms even help create new land, such as coral building reefs.

Contributing to Human Wellbeing: The ocean has a restorative effect, calming and connecting us. The positive impact it can have on our wellbeing is immense.

Understanding the importance of marine life is essential for ensuring its conservation and sustainable use4. It's crucial to remember that the behaviour and choices made by people seriously impact the wellbeing of our aquatic friends.

"My many years as a professional scuba diver have enabled me to visit and meet some of the wonderful inhabitants of our oceans. I have always felt privileged to witness the marvels I've encountered over the years. Continually educating myself about the fascinating aspects of the marine world is a journey I cherish. Happy learning!"

Jason

What can we do

Be mindful of your carbon footprint and work towards reducing energy consumption. You can lessen the impact of climate change on the ocean by being conscious of your energy use both at home and at work. Simple actions, such as switching to compact LED bulbs and opting for the stairs instead of the elevator, can make a significant difference. Every step counts!

Make Safe, Sustainable Seafood Choices: When shopping or dining out, help reduce the demand for over-exploited species by choosing seafood that is both healthful and sustainable.

Use Fewer Plastic Products: Plastics that end up as ocean debris contribute to habitat destruction and kill tens of thousands of marine animals each year. To limit your impact, carry a reusable water bottle, store food in non disposable containers, bring your own cloth tote or other reusable bag when shopping, and recycle whenever possible.

Help Take Care of the Beach: Always clean up after yourself when you enjoy diving, surfing, or relaxing on the beach. Encourage others to respect the marine environment or participate in local beach cleanups.

Don't Purchase Items That Exploit Marine Life: Avoid purchasing items such as coral jewellery, tortoiseshell hair accessories (made from hawks bill turtles), and other products.

Be an Ocean-Friendly Pet Owner: Consider seafood sustainability when choosing a diet for your pet. Never flush cat litter, which can contain pathogens harmful to marine life. Avoid stocking your aquarium with wild-caught saltwater fish.

Support Organisations Working to Protect the Ocean: Many institutes and organisations are fighting to protect ocean habitats and marine wildlife. Consider giving financial support or volunteering for hands-on work or advocacy.

Onto the Fun Stuff

Each page includes ten fascinating facts from the topic heading. Marine Biology from fish to plants to water to coral, by the time you finish this book, you will be able to answer questions that few people know the answers to, more complex as you delve deeper into the pages. Everyone loves a good fact. Interesting and some even mind blowing. Including creatures that are Alien. The exact number of species that live in the ocean is unknown.

However, scientists estimate that 91 percent of ocean species have yet to be classified. Current knowledge includes around 226,000 ocean species, but there could be as many as 700,000!

These species range from microscopic algae to the largest creature to have ever lived on Earth, the blue whale. The ocean has five major life zones, each with organisms uniquely adapted to their specific marine ecosystem, Lets jump in and learn.

Dolphins

1. Global Presence: Dolphins can be found all over the world and in different environments. There are 36 species of marine dolphins living in nearly all aquatic environments, including oceans, coastal, Earnestine and freshwater.

2. Freshwater Dolphins: The Amazon river is home to four species of river dolphin that are found nowhere else on Earth.

3. Speedsters: Bottle-nose dolphins are usually fairly slow swimmers, travelling at about 2 mph. However, they can reach speeds of over 30 mph for brief periods.

4. Communication: Dolphins have some of the most elaborate acoustic abilities in the animal kingdom. They make a variety of sounds including whistles, clicks, squawks, squeaks, moans, barks, groans and yelps.

5. Intelligence: Bottle-nose dolphins are one of the few species, along with apes and humans, that have the ability to recognise themselves in a mirror. This is considered 'reflective' of their intelligence.

6. Tool Use: Dolphins are also among the few animals that have been documented using tools. In Shark Bay in Western Australia, dolphins fit marine sponges over their beaks to protect them from sharp, harmful rocks as they forage for fish.

7. Sleep Pattern: Bottle-nose dolphins sleep with one half of their brain at a time, and keep one eye open.

8. Threats: Noise pollution from naval activity, the oil and gas industry, seismic surveys and underwater construction can stress and injure dolphins. It also severely interferes with their ability to communicate, reproduce, navigate and find prey.

9. Feeding Habits: Dolphins swallow a fish head first so the fish's spines don't catch in their throat.

10. Fishing Gear Threat: Bottle-nose dolphins are often killed accidentally in gillnets, driftnets, purse seines, trawls, long-lines and on hook-and-line gear used in fisheries.

Turtles

1. Ancient Creatures: Turtles have been around for over 200 million years, which means they lived alongside dinosaurs.

2. Part of the Skeleton: A turtle's shell, which grows with them throughout their lives, is actually part of its skeleton. It's made up of over 50 bones which include the turtle's rib cage and spine.

3. Can't Leave Their Shell: Contrary to popular belief, a turtle cannot come out of its shell. The turtle's shell grows with them, so it's impossible for them to grow too big for it.

4. Diverse Diet: What a turtle eats depends on the environment it lives in. Land-dwelling turtles will munch on beetles, fruit and grass, whereas sea dwellers will gobble everything from algae to squid and jellyfish.

5. Long Lifespan: Turtles can live to be over 100 years old.

6. Group Name: A group of turtles is called a Bale.

7. 'Lost Years': The first few years of a marine turtle's life are known as the 'lost years'. That's because the time between when the hatchlings emerge until they return to coastal shallow waters to forage is incredibly difficult to study.

8. Size Variation: Marine turtle species vary greatly in size. The smallest, Kemp's ridley, measure around 70cm long and weigh up to 40kg, whilst the leatherback can reach up to 180cm long and weigh 500kg.

9. Long Distance Migrants: Marine turtles can migrate incredibly long distances – the longest known record is for a female leatherback who swam nearly 13,000 miles over 647 days from Indonesia to the west coast of America.

10. Endangered Species: Sadly, many species of turtle are endangered! 129 of approximately 300 species of turtle and tortoise on Earth today are either vulnerable, endangered, or critically endangered.

Seawater

1. Covering the Earth: Around 70% of the planet's surface is covered by oceans. In fact, the oceans hold about 96.5% of all water on Earth.

2. Freezing Point: The freezing point of seawater lowers as the amount of salt dissolved in it increases. With average levels of salt, seawater freezes at -2 °C (28.4 °F).

3. Home to the Largest Ocean: The largest ocean on Earth is the Pacific Ocean, covering around 30% of the Earth's surface.

4. Longest Mountain Range: The longest mountain range in the world is found underwater. Stretching over 56,000km, the Mid-Oceanic Ridge is a mountain chain that runs along the centre of the ocean basins.

5. Oxygen Production: About 70% of the oxygen we breathe is produced by the oceans.

6. Home to the Largest Living Structure: The sea is home to the world's largest living structure – the Great Barrier Reef. Measuring around 2,600km, it can even be seen from the Moon!

7. Unexplored Territory: We have only explored about 5% of the world's oceans. There's a lot more to be discovered!

8. Historical Artefacts: The sea can be described as the planet's mega museum. There are more artefacts and remnants of history in the ocean than in all of the world's museums combined.

9. Water Weight: Water weighs about 8 pounds a gallon. Saltwater is heavier than freshwater.

10. Consistent Volume: There is about the same amount of water on Earth now as there was millions of years ago.

Freshwater V Saltwater

1. Freshwater is essential for all forms of life. It is a vital resource for all living organisms, playing a crucial role in sustaining ecosystems and supporting human civilisation.

2. Freshwater accounts for only a small fraction of the Earth's water. Despite covering about 70% of the Earth's surface, water bodies such as rivers, lakes, and groundwater constitute only about 2.5% of the planet's water.

3. Freshwater ecosystems are incredibly diverse. From serene lakes to meandering rivers and vibrant wetlands, freshwater ecosystems support a remarkable array of plant and animal species.

4. The water cycle sustains freshwater availability. The continuous movement of water through the water cycle ensures the replenishment of freshwater sources.

5. 68.7% of the fresh water on Earth is trapped in glaciers.

6. 30% of fresh water is in the ground.

7. 1.7% of the world's water is frozen and therefore unusable.

8. More than half of all fresh water on our planet seeps through soil and between rocks to form aquifers that are filled with groundwater.

9. The top surface of an aquifer is called the water table, and this is the depth where wells are drilled to bring fresh water into cities and homes.

10. Scientists who study freshwater ecosystems are called limnologists.

Strangest fish in the sea

1. Blood-red jellyfish: This mysterious red jelly may be a new species previously unknown to science. It likely belongs to the genus Poralia and was first spotted at a depth of around 2,300 feet just off the coast of Newport, Rhode Island.

2. Elusive glass octopus: This almost completely transparent creature, with only its cylindrical eyes, optic nerve, and digestive tract appearing opaque, was spotted by researchers from the Schmidt Ocean Institute in the deep sea of the Central Pacific Ocean.

3. Stonefish: The stonefish is the most venomous fish in the world.

4. Lion fish: The lionfish is amongst the most beautiful and unique fishes in the world.

5. Psychedelic Frogfish: The psychedelic frogfish is a peach-coloured frogfish.

6. Boxfish: The boxfish is box-shaped as the name suggests.

7. Frogfish: Frogfish are a type of anglerfish, known for their unique method of hunting. They use a lure that looks like a worm to attract prey.

8. Tassled Scorpionfish: The tassled scorpionfish is a master of camouflage, blending in with its surroundings to ambush prey.

9. Asian Sheepshead Wrasse: This fish is known for its large, bulbous forehead and its ability to change sex from female to male.

10. Fanfin Anglers: These deep-sea dwellers have a unique method of attracting prey. They have a bio-luminescent lure that they wave around to attract unsuspecting fish.

Blood-red Jellyfish

1. The blood-red jellyfish may be a new species previously unknown to science.

2. It was spotted about 2,300 feet underwater during an ambitious deep-ocean expedition.

3. The jellyfish has a blood-red body and appears to belong to the genus Poralia.

4. Only one other Poralia species has been described so far — Poralia rufescens, which has a bell-shaped body, 30 tentacles and lives in deep water across the world's oceans.

5. The NOAA team spotted the as-yet-unnamed jellyfish in footage from a deep-water dive conducted on July 28, off the coast of Newport, Rhode Island.

6. The agency's remotely operated vehicle (ROV) Deep Discoverer dove to a maximum depth of about 3,000 feet (915 m) into the North Atlantic Ocean, filming any creatures that it passed.

7. A variety of animals were seen during the dive, like ctenophores (also called comb jellies), cnidarians, crustaceans and Actinopterygii (ray-finned fishes).

8. The deep dive through the water column was part of NOAA's North Atlantic Stepping Stones expedition.

9. The team completed 25 dives, at depths ranging from 820 to 13,124 feet (250 to 4,000 m), in order to survey the elusive deep-sea creatures lurking in the area.

10. Some discoveries from the mission looked shockingly familiar. A few days earlier in the expedition, the team stumbled upon a yellow sea sponge lounging alongside a pink sea star some 6,184 feet (1,885 m) underwater

Glass Octopus

1. The glass octopus is nearly entirely transparent. Only its eyes, optic nerve, and digestive tract are opaque.

2. It is an incirrate octopus, belonging to the genus Vitreledonella and the family Amphitretidae.

3. The glass octopus is a transparent, gelatinous, and almost colourless meso- to bathypelagic octopod found worldwide in tropical and subtropical seas.

4. It has a mantle length up to 11 cm (4.3 in) and a total length up to 45 cm (18 in) in adults.

5. The upper three pairs of arms are subequal in length; in juveniles about as long as the mantle, in adults two to three times mantle length.

6. Male glass octopuses have a hectocotylised third left arm. This refers to when the male is ready to mate with a female, the arm can detach and release sperm to impregnate the female octopus.

7. The glass octopus's eyes are cylindrical to help camouflage them from their enemies.

8. The radula is heterodont, also known as heteroglossan, in which the middle or rhachidian tooth in each array has multiple cusps and the lateral teeth are unicuspid.

9. The glass octopus is ovoviviparous. The female broods her eggs, of which hundreds are within the mantle cavity.

10. Sightings of the glass octopus are incredibly rare. So rare over 34 days, researchers managed to get two sightings of the glass octopus deep down in the ocean, near the remote Phoenix Islands.

Stonefish

1. Stonefish are the most venomous fish in the world. Their venom is lethal both to other marine animals and humans.

2. The venom comes from their 13 spines along their backs. At the base of each spine is a venom sac which are activated under pressure.Their venom is used for self-defence, not hunting.

3. They are masters of camouflage. Their skin, covered in patches of brown, yellow, orange, or red, along with a textured surface, allows them to blend in with their surroundings.

4. They attack their prey fast. They can catch and consume prey in as fast as 0.0015 seconds.

5. While stonefish are considered the most venomous fish in the world, there have been no recorded deaths from stonefish stings in Australia since European arrival. An antivenom developed in 1959 has further reduced the likelihood of death.

6. However, stonefish stings are still incredibly painful and can cause serious illness if not treated promptly. Many people are stung each year, and immediate medical attention is crucial

7. They are related to lionfish, as are Scorpionfish, Dwarf Lionfish

8. They are hunted by sea snakes, stingrays, eels, and sharks, all of which are able to eat the stonefish while avoiding its venomous effects.

9. Stonefish are primarily found in the coastal regions of the Indo-Pacific, including the waters of Australia, Asia, and the Pacific Islands.

10. Stonefish have a relatively short lifespan, typically living between 5 and 10 years in the wild. However, few stonefish survive to adulthood due to predation and environmental factors. Those that reach maturity can enjoy a decade of life lurking in the shallow waters of the Indian and Pacific Oceans.

Lion Fish

1. Lionfish are known for their maroon, white or black stripes, intricate fins, and venomous spiky extensions.

2. They inhabit coral reefs of the Pacific Ocean, as well as the Indian Ocean, and are capable of adapting to a wide range of environments that vary in temperature and depth.

3. There are 12 species of Lionfish, and 2 species, the red lionfish and the common lionfish are currently classified as invasive species.

4. Lionfish diet on small fish, invertebrates, and molluscs and have few natural predators due to the potential threat of their venomous spikes.

5. The lionfish is edible, and it has been said that they are quite delicious. However, due to their venomous spines, they need to be processed with care prior to being consumed.

6. Their dorsal fins are venomous. The 13 long fins that extend from the spine of the lionfish are venomous and used to deter predators.

7. They are fierce predators. Lionfish have been documented to hunt over 50 species of fish.

8. To accommodate their large appetites, they have enormous stomach capacities. A lionfish's stomach can expand up to 30 times its regular size.

9. Their scales have a unique shape. Lionfish have cycloid scales that are thin and oval-shaped with smooth edges.

10. They usually hunt at night. Lionfish are believed to be nocturnal creatures, preferring to hunt at night.

Psychedelic Frogfish

1. The Psychedelic Frogfish (Histiophryne psychedelica) is a yellow-brown or peach-coloured frogfish named for its pink and white stripes arranged in a fingerprint pattern.

2. It was first described in 2009 by Pietsch, Arnold, and Hall in the scientific journal Copeia.

3. The fish is from waters near Ambon Island and Bali, Indonesia.

4. It has been known to reach a length of 15 centimetres (5.9 in).

5. The skin of the Psychedelic Frogfish is flabby and fleshy, like other frogfishes.

6. As a member of the order Lophiiformes, it has no scales.

7. The skin covers the dorsal and ventral fins of the fish, which aid in camouflaging the fish.

8. It has a tiny luring appendage on its forehead.

9. The colouring of the skin is a pattern of yellowish brown or peach-coloured stripes.

10. The fingerprint pattern, like the stripes on a zebra or the spots on a humpback whale's tail, is unique to each individual.

Box Fish

1. Boxfish have an exoskeleton: Boxfish have a special triangular or cube-shaped carapace exoskeleton made of bony plates that provides protection and gives them their unique shape.

2. Young boxfish are more round in shape: Most adults are generally square or triangular in shape, but young boxfish have softer, more rounded shapes.

3. They are slow swimmers: Their shape makes them slow swimmers; they are, however, highly manoeuvrable.

4. Some boxfish are very poisonous: They are all poisonous to eat to some extent. When it comes to human consumption, some species are a no-no, some have to be very carefully prepared.

5. Yellow boxfish lose their colour as they age: Yellow boxfish are known for their bright yellow colour. Younger individuals have a more striking bright yellow coloration, which starts to fade as they age.

6. Some release strong toxins when threatened: As part of their defensive mechanism, boxfish can release toxins (to various degrees of strength depending on the species).

7. Some boxfish have horns: Not all boxfish have horns. Some species of boxfish, such as the Cowfish and the Horned Boxfish, have horns or spines on their head.

8. Boxfish are carnivorous: They mostly feed on small invertebrates such as crustaceans and molluscs.

9. Boxfish reproduce by laying eggs: The eggs are fertilised externally; the eggs are then left to float in the water, where they hatch into larvae.

10. Boxfish are native to tropical and subtropical waters: They are found in the Atlantic, Indian, and Pacific oceans.

Frogfish

1. Master of Disguise: Frogfish are the ultimate camouflage artists of the underwater world. They can change their colour and texture to blend seamlessly with their surroundings, making them nearly invisible to both prey and predators.

2. Lures for Lunch: Frogfish have a unique way of hunting. They possess a modified dorsal spine called an "illicium" that resembles a fishing rod. At the end of this rod is a fleshy lure called an "esca" that they wiggle to attract unsuspecting prey.

3. Lightning-Fast Strike: Despite their sluggish appearance, frogfish are capable of the fastest strike of any vertebrate on Earth. They can engulf their prey in a matter of milliseconds, making it impossible for the victim to escape.

4. Walking on Fins: Frogfish lack a swim bladder, which helps most fish control their buoyancy. Instead, they "walk" along the seafloor using their pectoral fins, which resemble legs.

5. Ambush Predators: Frogfish are ambush predators, meaning they lie in wait for their prey to come to them. They are incredibly patient and can remain motionless for hours, waiting for the perfect opportunity to strike.

6. Voracious Appetite: Frogfish are not picky eaters and will attempt to eat anything that comes close to their lure, even if it's larger than themselves. They have expandable stomachs that allow them to swallow prey up to twice their size.

7. Variety of Shapes and Sizes: Frogfish come in a wide array of shapes, sizes, and colours. Some species resemble algae or coral, while others look like sponges or rocks. This diversity allows them to thrive in various habitats.

8. Cannibalistic Tendencies: Frogfish are known to be cannibalistic and will sometimes eat other frogfish, including members of their own species. This behaviour is more common in crowded environments where food is scarce.

9. No Teeth, No Problem: Frogfish lack teeth, so they swallow their prey whole. They have powerful digestive juices that break down the food in their stomachs.

10. Unique Reproductive Behaviour: Male frogfish attach themselves to the female's body. The female then lays the eggs in a gelatinous mass, which the male guards until they hatch.

Tassled Scorpionfish

1. Elaborate Camouflage: Tassled Scorpionfish are masters of disguise. Their bodies are adorned with colourful blotches and numerous tassels that resemble seaweed, making them incredibly difficult to spot against the reef.

2. Venomous Spines: This species possesses 18 venomous spines – 13 on their dorsal fin, 3 on their anal fin, and 2 on their pelvic fins. Their sting is incredibly painful and can cause swelling, nausea, and even paralysis in humans.

3. Patient Hunters: Tassled Scorpionfish are ambush predators. They lie motionless on the reef, waiting for unsuspecting prey to swim by. Their camouflage helps them blend in seamlessly with their surroundings, making them the perfect hunters.

4. Lightning-Fast Strike: When a meal comes close, the Tassled Scorpionfish strikes with incredible speed. They open their large mouths and create a powerful suction, inhaling their prey in a matter of milliseconds.

5. Diverse Diet: These fish have a varied diet, primarily feeding on small fish and crustaceans that inhabit the reef. They are opportunistic feeders and will eat almost anything they can fit in their mouths.

6. Nocturnal Nature: Tassled Scorpionfish are primarily nocturnal creatures. They spend most of the day hiding in crevices and under ledges, emerging at night to hunt.

7. Wide Distribution: This species is found throughout the Indo-Pacific region, from the Red Sea to the coast of Africa and across to the Pacific Islands. They inhabit coral reefs, rocky areas, and seaweed beds.

8. Solitary Lifestyle: Tassled Scorpionfish are solitary creatures, only coming together to mate. They are not territorial and will tolerate other individuals of their species in their vicinity.

9. Long Lifespan: These fish can live for up to 20 years in the wild. They are slow-growing and late to mature, which makes them vulnerable to overfishing and habitat destruction.

10. Important Role in the Ecosystem: As predators, Tassled Scorpionfish play a crucial role in maintaining the balance of the reef ecosystem. They help control populations of smaller fish and crustaceans, preventing them from overgrazing on algae and coral.

Asian Sheepshead Wrasse

1. Giant Wrasse: The Asian Sheepshead Wrasse, or Kobudai, is one of the largest wrasse species, reaching up to 3.3 feet (1 meter) in length.

2. Distinctive Features: They sport a prominent bulge on their forehead and a thick lower lip, giving them a unique appearance.

3. Sex Change: Kobudai are sequential hermaphrodites, starting as females and transforming into males later in life, often triggered by social cues.

4. Habitat: They inhabit rocky reefs in the western Pacific Ocean, primarily around Japan, Korea, and China.

5. Diet: Kobudai are opportunistic predators, feeding on a variety of shellfish, crustaceans, and small fish.

6. Powerful Jaws: Their strong jaws and teeth allow them to crush the shells of their prey with ease. Its large, fang-like teeth allow it to crack open hard shells with ease, making it an adept predator of crustaceans, molluscs, and sea urchins

7. Social Structure: These fish form harems, with one dominant male presiding over a group of females. This arrangement ensures reproductive success and maintains stability within their underwater communities.

8. Long Lifespan: Kobudai can live for several decades, with some individuals estimated to be over 50 years old.

9. Conservation Status: Due to overfishing and habitat destruction, the Asian Sheepshead Wrasse is listed as endangered by the IUCN.

10. Cultural Significance: In Japan, Kobudai are considered a delicacy and are highly prized for their flavorful meat. Please don't join the trend!

Fanfin Anglers

1. Deep-Sea Dwellers: Fanfin Anglers are found in the dark depths of the ocean, typically at depths of 3,000 to 8,000 feet (900 to 2,400 meters).

2. Bioluminescent Lure: They possess a bioluminescent lure at the tip of a modified dorsal spine, used to attract prey in the light-less abyss.

3. Extreme Sexual Dimorphism: Male Fanfin Anglers are significantly smaller than females and often attach themselves to the female's body as parasites, fusing their tissues and becoming dependent on her for nourishment.

4. Globular Shape: Their bodies are globular and gelatinous, lacking scales and possessing a large mouth filled with sharp teeth.

5. Ambush Predators: Fanfin Anglers are ambush predators, patiently waiting for unsuspecting prey to be attracted to their glowing lure before quickly engulfing them.

6. Diverse Species: There are numerous species of Fanfin Anglers, each with unique adaptations to their specific habitat and prey.

7. Rarely Seen: Due to their deep-sea habitat and elusive nature, Fanfin Anglers are rarely encountered by humans and remain mysterious creatures of the deep.

8. Adaptations to Pressure: Their bodies are adapted to withstand the immense pressure of the deep sea, with gelatinous tissues and flexible skeletons.

9. Slow Metabolism: Fanfin Anglers have a slow metabolism, allowing them to survive long periods without food in the sparsely populated depths.

10. Important Role in Ecosystem: They play a vital role in the deep-sea food web, serving as both predators and prey, contributing to the balance of this unique ecosystem.

eels

1. Diverse Species: There are over 800 species of eels found in saltwater oceans, including moray eels, conger eels, and snake eels.

2. Global Distribution: Saltwater eels inhabit oceans worldwide, from tropical reefs to deep-sea environments.

3. Elongated Bodies: Eels have long, cylindrical bodies that resemble snakes, allowing them to navigate through tight spaces and burrows.

4. Carnivorous Diet: Most saltwater eels are carnivorous predators, feeding on fish, crustaceans, and other marine organisms.

5. Nocturnal Behaviour: Many saltwater eels are nocturnal, hunting and feeding under the cover of darkness.

6. Hidden Habitats: Saltwater eels often hide in crevices, reefs, and rocky areas, ambushing prey that comes too close.

7. Electric Shock: Some species of saltwater eels, like the electric eel, can produce powerful electric shocks to stun prey and defend themselves.

8. Spawning Migration: Some saltwater eels, like the American and European eels, undertake long migrations to specific spawning grounds in the ocean.

9. Larval Stage: Eel eggs hatch into transparent, leaf-like larvae called leptocephalus, which drift in ocean currents for months before transforming into adult eels.

10. Important Ecological Role: Saltwater eels play an essential role in marine ecosystems by controlling prey populations and serving as food for larger predators.

Strange Crabs

1. Decorator Crabs: These crabs camouflage themselves with sponges, algae, and other debris for protection. They even replace the decorations as they grow!

2. Pom-Pom Crabs: These tiny crabs carry anemones in their claws like cheerleaders with pom-poms. The anemones sting predators and the crabs get scraps of food.

3. Boxer Crabs: These crabs wield anemones in their claws like boxing gloves, punching and stinging anything that comes too close.

4. Arrowhead Crabs: These bizarre crabs have elongated, arrow-shaped bodies and extremely long legs, making them resemble spiders more than crabs.

5. Sponge Crabs: These crabs carve out living sponges and wear them as portable shelters, blending in perfectly with their surroundings.

6. Pea Crabs: These tiny crabs live as parasites inside oysters, mussels, and other bivalves, feeding on their host's filtered food.

7. Horseshoe Crabs: These ancient creatures are not true crabs but are more closely related to spiders and scorpions. Their blue blood is used in medical testing.

8. Coconut Crabs: These giant land crabs are the largest terrestrial arthropods on Earth. They can climb trees, crack coconuts with their powerful claws, and even steal shiny objects.

9. Yeti Crabs: These deep-sea crabs are covered in silky, hair-like bristles that they use to farm bacteria for food in the extreme environment.

10. Ghost Crabs: These nocturnal crabs have pale bodies and incredible speed, allowing them to disappear into the sand like ghosts.

Flying Fish

1. Not True Flight: Flying fish don't actually fly like birds or bats. Instead, they use their powerful pectoral fins to glide above the water's surface.

2. Extended Glides: They can glide for considerable distances, sometimes up to 400 meters, and reach heights of several meters above the water.

3. Escape Mechanism: Their gliding ability is primarily a defence mechanism to evade predators like tuna, dolphin, and marlin.

4. Warm Water Habitats: Flying fish are found in tropical and subtropical oceans around the world, preferring warmer waters.

5. Diverse Species: There are over 60 different species of flying fish, each with slightly different characteristics and gliding abilities.

6. Speed Demons: They can reach speeds of up to 70 kilometres per hour (43 mph) underwater before launching themselves into the air.

7. Lifespan: Flying fish typically live for around 5 years, though some species may have shorter or longer lifespans.

8. Attraction to Light: They are attracted to light, which sometimes leads them to accidentally land on boats at night.

9. Diet: Flying fish primarily feed on plankton and small crustaceans, filtering them from the water.

10. Important Prey: They are an important food source for larger predators in the ocean, playing a crucial role in the marine food web.

Sunlight & Water

1. The Sunlight Zone: The top layer of the ocean, where sunlight penetrates, is called the euphotic zone or sunlight zone. This zone extends to a depth of about 200 meters (656 feet).

2. Colour Absorption: As sunlight enters the water, it is absorbed and scattered. Red light is absorbed first, followed by orange, yellow, green, and violet. This is why the ocean appears blue at depth.

3. Twilight Zone: Below the sunlight zone lies the twilight zone (disphotic zone), where only a faint amount of light reaches. This zone extends to about 1,000 meters (3,280 feet).

4. Midnight Zone: Below the twilight zone is the midnight zone (aphotic zone), where sunlight does not penetrate at all. This zone makes up the vast majority of the ocean's depth.

5. Bioluminescence: In the absence of sunlight, many deep-sea creatures produce their own light through bioluminescence, using it for communication, attracting prey, and camouflage.

6. Photosynthesis: Sunlight in the euphotic zone is essential for phytoplankton, microscopic plants that form the base of the marine food web and produce a significant portion of the Earth's oxygen.

7. Temperature Gradient: Sunlight also influences the ocean's temperature. The surface layers are warmer due to solar heating, while the deeper layers remain cold.

8. Deep-Sea Adaptations: Creatures living in the deep ocean have evolved unique adaptations to cope with the absence of sunlight, such as large eyes, bioluminescence, and slow metabolisms.

9. Underwater Visibility: Sunlight affects underwater visibility, with clearer water in the sunlight zone and decreasing visibility with depth due to light scattering and absorption.

10. Sunburn for Divers: Sunlight can penetrate the water's surface, so divers can get sunburned even when submerged, especially in shallow water or when spending extended periods near the surface.

Starfish

1. Starfish are not actually fish, but echinoderms, closely related to sea urchins and sand dollars. The common starfish (also known as the common sea star or sugar starfish) is the most familiar starfish in the north-east Atlantic. It belongs to the family Asteriidae and typically has five arms, growing to between 10–30 cm across, although larger specimens (up to 52 cm across) are known. These starfish are usually orange or brownish in colour, sometimes violet, and can be found on rocky and gravelly substrates where they feed on molluscs and other benthic invertebrates

2. They have no brain or central nervous system, but a network of nerves that help them sense their surroundings.

3. Their eyes are located at the tips of their arms, allowing them to detect light and dark.

4. They move using hundreds of tiny tube feet filled with seawater, which create suction to grip surfaces.

5. Starfish can regenerate lost arms, and some species can even regrow an entire body from a single arm.

6. They have a fascinating feeding mechanism. They extend their stomachs out of their mouths and wrap them around their prey, such as molluscs and other benthic invertebrates. This external digestion allows them to break down their food before retracting their stomachs back into their bodies.

7. Some starfish species are venomous, using their spines to inject toxins into predators or prey.

8. They come in a wide variety of shapes, sizes, and colours, with some species having up to 50 arms.

9. Starfish are found in all of the world's oceans, from shallow tide pools to the deep sea.

10. They play a crucial role in maintaining the health of marine ecosystems, controlling populations of mussels and other shellfish.

Sharks

1. Ancient Mariners: Sharks predate dinosaurs, having roamed the oceans for over 400 million years! Their cartilaginous skeletons rarely fossilise, but their teeth tell tales of prehistoric seas.

2. Electrifying Senses: Sharks possess a "sixth sense" - electroreception. They detect the faintest electrical fields generated by muscle contractions of hidden prey. Imagine feeling a heartbeat from meters away!

3. Living Fossils: Some species, like the frilled shark, are virtually unchanged from their ancestors millions of years ago. They're deep-sea dwellers, rarely seen and shrouded in mystery.

4. Never-Ending Smile: A shark can lose over 30,000 teeth in its lifetime! Don't worry, rows of replacements are ready to take their place, ensuring a perpetual toothy grin.

5. Diverse Family: There are over 500 known shark species! They range from the tiny dwarf lanternshark, barely longer than your finger, to the colossal whale shark, the largest fish in the sea.

6. Masters of Disguise: Wobbegong sharks are masters of camouflage, resembling a seaweed-covered rock. They lie in wait, ambushing unsuspecting prey with lightning-fast strikes.

7. Deep Divers: Sharks can plunge to astonishing depths. The Portuguese dogfish dives over 3.5 kilometres (2.2 miles) below the surface, venturing into a realm of crushing pressure and perpetual darkness.

8. Speed Demons: The shortfin mako shark is a Formula One racer of the ocean, clocking speeds up to 74 kilometres (46 miles) per hour! Its streamlined body and powerful tail propel it through the water with ease.

9. Gender Bender: Some shark species, like the blacktip reef shark, can reproduce asexually! Females can give birth to genetically identical offspring without mating, an evolutionary insurance policy.

10. Super Swimmers: Sharks are incredibly efficient swimmers. Their unique skin, covered in tiny tooth-like scales called denticles, reduces drag and allows them to glide effortlessly through the water.

Strange Coral

1. Bubble Coral (Plerogyra sinuosa): This coral appears to have inflated bubbles or balloons on its surface during the day, but at night, it extends its tentacles to feed, creating a dramatic transformation.

2. Brain Coral (Faviidae): Its surface features intricate grooves and ridges resembling the folds of a human brain. Some colonies can live for centuries, slowly expanding their massive structures.

3. Mushroom Coral (Fungia spp.): Unlike most corals attached to the reef, this solitary species resembles a mushroom cap and can move across the ocean floor.

4. Venus Flytrap Anemone (Actinoscyphia aurelia): Though not technically a coral, this deep-sea creature mimics the carnivorous plant with its tentacles resembling the trap's lobes, capturing prey.

5. Wire Coral (Cirrhipathes spp.):** Instead of a typical branching structure, this coral grows in long, thin filaments, resembling a tangled web of wires swaying in the current.

6. Sun Coral (Tubastraea spp.):** Unique among corals, it lacks zooxanthellae, the symbiotic algae that provide most corals with their vibrant colors and energy. It feeds on plankton instead.

7. Elkhorn Coral (Acropora palmata):** This branching coral forms dense thickets resembling elk antlers. Once abundant in the Caribbean, it's now critically endangered due to climate change and disease.

8. Lettuce Coral (Agaricia agaricites):** Its broad, leafy fronds resemble a head of lettuce. It can fluoresce under certain lighting conditions, emitting a vibrant green glow.

9. Torch Coral (Euphyllia glabrescens):** This coral extends long, flowing tentacles that resemble a flaming torch. It can deliver a painful sting to protect its territory.

10. Red Whip Coral (Leptogorgia virgulata):** This soft coral lacks a hard skeleton. Its colonies grow in long, whip-like strands, creating underwater forests that sway gracefully in the current.

Oysters

1. Gender Fluidity: Oysters can change their sex multiple times throughout their lives, starting as males and often transitioning to females as they mature.

2. Filter Power: A single oyster can filter up to 50 gallons of water per day, removing pollutants and excess nutrients, playing a crucial role in maintaining water quality.

3. Ancient History: Oysters have been around for over 15 million years, and their fossils reveal insights into prehistoric ecosystems and climate change.

4. Living Rocks: Oyster reefs are not just clusters of shells; they are living structures that provide habitat for countless marine species, enhancing biodiversity.

5. Silent Scream: While lacking a central nervous system, oysters can sense changes in their environment, reacting to light, touch, and chemicals. Some even exhibit a "startle response" when threatened.

6. Pearl Power: Not all oysters produce pearls, and those that do create them as a defence mechanism against irritants. The rarest and most valuable pearls are formed naturally, without human intervention.

7. Ancient Aphrodisiac: Oysters have long been considered an aphrodisiac due to their high zinc content, which is essential for testosterone production.

8. Taste of Place: Oysters from different regions have distinct flavors influenced by the water's salinity, temperature, and the type of algae they consume.

9. Shell Shock: Oyster shells are not waste; they are valuable resources used to create reefs, improve water quality, and even supplement animal feed.

10. Living Fossils: Some oyster species can live for decades, with the oldest recorded specimen reaching over 50 years old. These ancient molluscs offer a glimpse into the past and hold secrets of survival in a changing world.

Sea Snakes

1. Paddle Power: Sea snakes have flattened, paddle-like tails for efficient swimming, making them graceful underwater dancers.

2. Lung Divers: While they need to breathe air, some sea snakes can hold their breath for up to two hours, allowing them to hunt at depths where most predators can't reach.

3. Venomous But Not Vicious: Sea snakes possess potent venom, but they are generally docile and only bite when threatened or accidentally caught in fishing nets.

4. Salty Sippers: They have specialised glands near their tongues that allow them to drink seawater and excrete excess salt through their nostrils.

5. Skin Breathers: Some sea snake species can absorb up to 33% of their oxygen needs directly through their skin, extending their dive time.

6. Live Birth Givers: Unlike most snakes that lay eggs, all sea snakes give birth to live young underwater.

7. Colour Chameleons: Sea snakes come in a variety of colours and patterns, from banded and striped to solid hues, providing camouflage in their inverse habitats.

8. Depth Defiers: Some species can dive as deep as 250 meters (820 feet) to hunt for their prey, braving the cold and darkness of the ocean depths.

9. Sensory Specialists: They have specialised scales on their bellies that detect vibrations in the water, helping them locate prey and avoid predators.

10. Evolving Enigma: Sea snakes are a relatively young group of reptiles, having evolved from land-dwelling snakes only about 10 million years ago, making them a fascinating example of adaptation.

Whales

1. Vocal Virtuosos: Humpback whales are known for their complex songs, which can last for hours and be heard for miles underwater. These songs are believed to play a role in mating and social communication.

2. Deep Divers: Sperm whales are the deepest diving mammals, capable of plunging to depths of over 3,000 meters (9,800 feet) in search of giant squid.

3. Blowing Giants: The spray from a blue whale's blowhole can reach a height of 9 meters (30 feet), making it visible from miles away.

4. Ancient Mariners: Bowhead whales are the longest-living mammals, with some individuals estimated to be over 200 years old.

5. Gentle Giants: Despite their massive size, baleen whales feed on tiny organisms like krill, filtering them through their baleen plates.

6. Navigational Experts: Gray whales undertake the longest annual migration of any mammal, travelling up to 22,000 kilometres (13,700 miles) between their feeding and breeding grounds.

7. Social Butterflies: Orcas, also known as killer whales, are highly intelligent and social animals that live in complex family groups called pods.

8. Echolocation Masters: Toothed whales use echolocation, a biological sonar, to navigate, find food, and communicate in the darkness of the ocean depths.

9. Cultural Transmission: Some whale populations have distinct dialects or behaviours that are passed down through generations, suggesting a form of cultural learning.

10. Endangered Giants: Many whale species are still recovering from past over-hunting, and some, like the North Atlantic right whale, face a critical risk of extinction.

Bowhead Whales

1. Icebreakers: Bowhead whales use their massive, bow-shaped skulls to break through Arctic ice up to 60 cm (2 feet) thick, creating breathing holes and access to feeding areas.

2. Vocal Communicators: They produce a wide range of sounds, including calls, whistles, and moans, used for communication, navigation, and potentially even cultural transmission.

3. Long-Lived Leviathans: Bowhead whales are among the longest-living mammals on Earth, with some individuals estimated to be over 200 years old, bearing witness to centuries of environmental change.

4. Thick-Skinned Survivors: They possess the thickest blubber of any animal, reaching up to 50 cm (20 inches), providing insulation against the frigid Arctic waters.

5. Gentle Giants: Despite their immense size, bowhead whales are primarily filter feeders, consuming vast quantities of tiny crustaceans called copepods using their baleen plates.

6. Cultural Icons: Bowhead whales hold deep cultural significance for Indigenous communities in the Arctic, who have relied on them for sustenance and cultural practices for millennia.

7. Resilient Survivors: They have rebounded from near extinction due to commercial whaling in the 19th and 20th centuries, demonstrating their remarkable ability to adapt and thrive in challenging environments.

8. Deep Divers: While primarily found in shallow waters, bowhead whales are capable of diving to depths of over 200 meters (656 feet) to forage for food or evade predators.

9. Mysterious Migrations: Their migration patterns remain partially understood, with some individuals undertaking long journeys through icy waters while others remain in specific regions year-round.

10. Arctic Architects: Bowhead whales play a crucial role in their ecosystem, creating and maintaining open water areas through their ice-breaking activities, benefiting other marine species.

Krill

1. Shrink and Grow: Krill have the remarkable ability to shrink their bodies during periods of food scarcity and then regrow when food becomes abundant again.

2. Bioluminescent Balter: They possess bioluminescent organs, producing light displays for communication and potentially confusing predators.

3. Swarm Intelligence: Krill swarms exhibit collective behaviour, forming massive, synchronised groups that can span kilometres and contain billions of individuals.

4. Carbon Capture Crusaders: They play a crucial role in the global carbon cycle, consuming carbon-rich phytoplankton and transporting it to the depths through their fecal pellets.

5. Deep-Sea Nursery: Krill eggs sink to great depths, where the larvae develop before migrating upward to join the surface swarms.

6. Age-Defying Masters: Determining the age of krill is challenging due to their molting process, making it difficult to assess their lifespan accurately.

7. Chemical Communication: They release pheromones to signal danger or attract mates, creating complex chemical communication networks within their swarms.

8. Evolutionary Marvels: Krill have evolved unique adaptations for life in the Southern Ocean, including specialised filtering appendages and antifreeze proteins.

9. Nutritional Powerhouses: Packed with omega-3 fatty acids, antioxidants, and other essential nutrients, making them a vital food source for marine animals and a potential resource for human consumption.

10. Genetic Diversity Hotspots: Krill populations exhibit high genetic diversity, which may contribute to their resilience in the face of environmental change.

Who Eats the krill

1. Baleen Whales: The largest animals on Earth, including blue, humpback, and fin whales, rely heavily on krill as their primary food source.

2. Penguins: Adelie, chinstrap, and gentoo penguins in Antarctica depend on krill to feed their chicks and sustain themselves during the harsh winter months.

3. Seals: Crabeater seals are specially adapted to consume krill, with sieve-like teeth that filter the tiny crustaceans from the water. Leopard seals also prey on krill, among other animals.

4. Fish: Many fish species, such as lanternfish and herring, feed on krill, forming an essential link in the marine food web.

5. Seabirds: Petrels, albatrosses, and other seabirds swoop down to the ocean surface to scoop up krill, providing a crucial source of energy for their long flights.

6. Squid: Several squid species, including the colossal squid, include krill in their diet, particularly in deeper waters where other prey is scarce.

7. Other Crustaceans: Larger crustaceans, like krill-eating amphipods, feed on krill, creating a complex predator-prey relationship within their ecosystem.

8. Jellyfish: Some jellyfish species consume krill, although they are not a primary food source for these gelatinous creatures.

9. Humans: Krill are increasingly harvested for human consumption, mainly as a dietary supplement due to their high omega-3 fatty acid content.

10. The Circle of Life: Krill are decomposed by bacteria and other microbes after death, returning nutrients to the ecosystem and supporting the growth of phytoplankton, which krill then feed on, completing the cycle.

Squid

1. Masters of Disguise: Squids are chameleons of the sea, able to change their skin colour and texture in the blink of an eye to camouflage with their surroundings or communicate with each other.

2. Jet-Powered Propulsion: They are jet-propelled swimmers, using a powerful siphon to expel water and rocket through the ocean at speeds of up to 25 miles per hour.

3. Three Hearts, One Mind: Squids have three hearts – two branchial hearts that pump blood through the gills and one systemic heart that circulates blood throughout the body.

4. Giant Eyes: The colossal squid boasts the largest eyes in the animal kingdom, each measuring up to 12 inches in diameter, allowing them to detect prey in the dim depths.

5. Ink Masters: When threatened, squids release a cloud of ink to confuse predators, giving them a chance to escape. This ink was once used as writing ink.

6. Brainy Cephalopods: Squids are considered among the most intelligent invertebrates, exhibiting complex problem-solving skills and social behaviours.

7. Arms and Tentacles: They have eight arms lined with suckers for grasping prey, and two longer tentacles with hooks for snagging and securing food.

8. Beak of Steel: Hidden within their arms is a sharp, parrot-like beak used to tear apart their prey, which includes fish, crustaceans, and even other squids.

9. Deep-Sea Dwellers: Some squid species live in the abyssal depths, over 3,000 meters (9,800 feet) below the surface, where sunlight never reaches.

10. Ancient Origins: Squid fossils dating back over 300 million years have been discovered, revealing their long and fascinating evolutionary history.

Cuttlefish

1. Colour-Changing Masters: Cuttlefish are the chameleons of the sea, able to change their skin colour and pattern in a fraction of a second for camouflage, communication, and even hypnosis of prey.

2. W-Shaped Pupils: Their unique W-shaped pupils allow for panoramic vision and exceptional depth perception, even in low-light conditions.

3. Three Hearts, Blue Blood: They possess three hearts to pump their copper-based blue blood, a highly efficient oxygen carrier.

4. Internal Buoyancy Control: Cuttlefish have a cuttlebone, a gas-filled internal shell, that allows them to precisely control their buoyancy and hover effortlessly in the water.

5. Masterful Mimics: They can imitate the shape and texture of objects in their environment, such as seaweed or rocks, to avoid detection.

6. Hypnotic Hunters: Some cuttlefish species use mesmerising displays of flashing colours and patterns to disorient prey before capturing them with lightning-fast tentacles.

7. Ingenious Ink: When threatened, they release a cloud of ink that not only creates a visual smokescreen but also contains chemicals that can irritate and confuse predators.

8. Walking Wonders: Juvenile cuttlefish can "walk" along the seafloor using their arms, a behaviour rarely seen in cephalopods.

9. Gender-Bending Tactics: Males can disguise themselves as females to sneak past rival males and mate with females unnoticed.

10. Internal Ink Factory: They produce their ink internally in a specialised organ, ensuring a constant supply for defence and deception.

Shrimp

1. Heart in the Head: Shrimp have their hearts located in their heads! This peculiar anatomy allows for efficient blood circulation throughout their bodies.

2. Born Male, Become Female: Most shrimp species are protandric hermaphrodites, meaning they start life as males and then transform into females later in life.

3. Backward Swimmers: Shrimp don't swim forward like fish. Instead, they propel themselves backward by flexing their abdomens and tails.

4. Transparent Exoskeleton: Their translucent exoskeleton allows them to blend in with their surroundings, making them masters of camouflage.

5. Sonic Blasters: Pistol shrimp possess a specialised claw that can create a cavitation bubble, producing a sonic blast louder than a jet engine and stunning prey.

6. Ancient Lineage: Shrimp have been around for hundreds of millions of years, with fossil evidence dating back to the Devonian period.

7. Diverse Diets: They are opportunistic feeders, consuming algae, plankton, dead organisms, and even small fish, depending on the species and availability.

8. Global Delicacy: Shrimp are one of the most popular seafood's worldwide, enjoyed in various culinary traditions and preparations.

9. Environmental Indicators: Their sensitivity to pollution makes them valuable bioindicators, helping scientists monitor water quality and ecosystem health.

10. Social Cleaners: Some shrimp species have symbiotic relationships with fish, acting as "cleaners" by removing parasites and dead skin from their hosts.

The Almighty Pistol Shrimp

1. Sonic Boom: Pistol shrimp produce one of the loudest sounds in the ocean with their specialised claw, creating a cavitation bubble that generates a sonic blast reaching over 200 decibels.

2. Bubble Bullet: This sonic blast isn't just noise; it creates a high-pressure bubble that collapses violently, stunning or killing prey with a shock wave.

3. Fastest Claw in the West: The pistol shrimp's claw snaps shut at an astonishing speed of 60 miles per hour, faster than a bullet from a .22 calibre rifle.

4. Hotter Than the Sun: The collapsing cavitation bubble briefly reaches temperatures hotter than the surface of the sun, creating a flash of light visible to the naked eye.

5. Symbiotic Sharpshooters: Some species of pistol shrimp live in symbiosis with goby fish, who act as lookouts while the shrimp maintain their shared burrow.

6. Underwater Architects: Pistol shrimp are skilled burrowers, constructing complex tunnels and chambers in the sand or mud, where they live and ambush prey.

7. Variety is the Spice of Life: There are over 600 known species of pistol shrimp, each with its unique claw shape, size, and sonic abilities.

8. Tiny but Mighty: Despite their small size, typically measuring less than an inch long, pistol shrimp pack a powerful punch with their sonic weaponry.

9. Reef Protectors: Their sonic blasts help deter predators and maintain the balance of reef ecosystems by controlling populations of smaller organisms.

10. Research Inspiration: Pistol shrimp have inspired advancements in technology, including the development of bio-inspired materials and underwater communication systems.

Leafy Seadragon

1. Masters of Disguise: Leafy seadragons are experts at camouflage, blending seamlessly with seaweed and kelp forests thanks to their leaf-like appendages.

2. Slow Movers: They are not strong swimmers, relying on their camouflage and slow movements to avoid predators.

3. Dancing Courtship: Leafy seadragons engage in elaborate courtship rituals, including a graceful dance where the male and female mirror each others movements.

4. Egg-Carrying Dads: The male leafy seadragon is responsible for carrying and incubating the eggs. The female deposits them onto a specialised brood patch on the male's tail.

5. Independent Babies: After hatching, the juvenile leafy seadragons are completely independent, fending for themselves without any parental care.

6. Picky Eaters: Their diet consists mainly of mysid shrimp, which they suck up with their pipette-like snouts.

7. Endangered Species: Leafy seadragons are protected by law in Australia, as their populations are threatened by habitat loss, pollution, and illegal collection for the aquarium trade.

8. Australian Natives: They are only found in the waters surrounding southern and western Australia, making them a unique and iconic symbol of the region's marine biodiversity.

9. Living Fossils: Leafy seadragons are considered living fossils, with their lineage dating back millions of years. They offer valuable insights into the evolution of marine life.

10. Underwater Wonders: Their mesmerising appearance and unique behaviours make them a popular attraction for divers and underwater photographers, contributing to ecotourism efforts.

Pink See-Through Fantasia

1. Translucent Wonder: The Pink See-Through Fantasia is renowned for its completely transparent body, revealing its internal organs, including its digestive system.

2. Swimming Sea Cucumber: Unlike most sea cucumbers that crawl along the ocean floor, this species is a free-swimming marvel, using webbed structures for graceful underwater ballet.

3. Deep-Sea Dweller: It inhabits the depths of the Celebes Sea in the western Pacific Ocean, typically found at depths of around 2,500 meters (8,200 feet).

4. Bioluminescent Defence: When threatened, the Pink See-Through Fantasia emits light from its body, potentially startling predators or attracting larger predators to scare off its attacker.

5. Filtering Feeder: It primarily feeds on marine snow, organic debris that drifts down from the surface, filtering it through its body for nourishment.

6. Elusive Discovery: This fascinating creature was only discovered in 2007 during the Census of Marine Life, a decade-long project exploring the ocean's biodiversity.

7. Size Range: Pink See-Through Fantasias can vary in size, with smaller individuals appearing bright pink and larger adults showcasing a darker reddish-brown hue.

8. Unique Breathing Method: Like other sea cucumbers, it breathes by drawing water into its anus and expelling it, absorbing oxygen through its respiratory trees in the process.

9. Gender Mystery: Little is known about their reproductive behaviour and whether they are hermaphrodites or have separate sexes.

10. Research Challenges: Due to their deep-sea habitat and elusive nature, studying Pink See-Through Fantasias poses challenges for scientists, leaving much to be discovered about their biology and behaviour.

Blobfish

1. Gelatinous Blob, Not a Blobby Fish: Blobfish are not actually as blobby as they appear in viral photos. Those images show them out of their natural habitat, where the lack of pressure causes their bodies to collapse and expand.

2. Deep-Sea Dweller: Blobfish live at depths of 600-1,200 meters (2,000-4,000 feet) off the coasts of Australia and New Zealand. At these depths, the pressure is immense, and the blobfish gelatinous body helps them maintain buoyancy.

3. Low-Energy Lifestyle: Due to the scarcity of food in the deep sea, blobfish have evolved to conserve energy. They have minimal muscle mass and primarily float along, waiting for prey to drift by.

4. Opportunistic Eaters: They primarily feed on small crustaceans, sea pens, and other invertebrates that float within their reach.

5. Parental Care: Female blobfish are dedicated mothers, guarding their eggs until they hatch and even sometimes cleaning them.

6. No Bones About It: Blobfish lack a true skeleton, which further contributes to their gelatinous appearance. Instead, they rely on the pressure of the deep sea to maintain their shape.

7. Ugliest Animal?: In 2013, the blobfish was voted the world's ugliest animal in an online poll. However, this is a subjective view, and many find them fascinating creatures.

8. Conservation Concerns: While not directly targeted by fishing, blobfish are sometimes caught as bycatch in deep-sea trawling, posing a potential threat to their populations.

9. Gelatinous Genome: Scientists are studying the blobfish unique physiology and genetics to better understand deep-sea adaptations and potentially discover new biomolecules.

10. Deep-Sea Ambassadors: Blobfish have become unlikely ambassadors for deep-sea conservation, raising awareness about the unique and fragile ecosystems that exist in the ocean's depths.

Sarcastic Fringehead

1. Big Mouth: Sarcastic fringeheads have disproportionately large mouths, capable of opening to an impressive width, exposing a vibrant yellow interior and sharp teeth.

2. Territorial Terrors: They are fiercely territorial, defending their chosen shelters (often burrows or crevices) with aggressive displays and threatening gaping mouths.

3. Kiss of War: When two fringeheads clash over territory, they engage in a "kissing" contest, pressing their open mouths against each other until one backs down.

4. Masters of Ambush: These fish are ambush predators, lurking in their hiding spots and lunging out to snatch unsuspecting prey with lightning speed.

5. Variety in Diet: Their diet is diverse, including small fish, crustaceans, and even squid eggs, especially during squid spawning season.

6. Colourful Personalities: While mostly brown or grey, male sarcastic fringeheads can display striking colours, such as black bodies with yellow jaws, during territorial disputes.

7. Egg Guardians: Females lay eggs in burrows or under rocks, and males fiercely guard them until they hatch, ensuring the survival of their offspring.

8. Homebodies: Sarcastic fringeheads are primarily found along the Pacific coast of North America, from San Francisco to Baja California, Mexico.

9. Shallow Dwellers: They typically inhabit shallow waters, often less than 30 meters (98 feet) deep, preferring rocky reefs and kelp forests.

10. Underappreciated Divers' Delight: Despite their intimidating appearance, sarcastic fringeheads are a fascinating sight for divers, offering a glimpse into the complex social behaviours and fierce territoriality of these underwater creatures. help

Goblin Shark

1. Living Fossil: The goblin shark is a living fossil, belonging to an ancient lineage of sharks that dates back over 125 million years.

2. Elusive Deep-Sea Dweller: Goblin sharks primarily inhabit the deep ocean, typically found at depths of 270 to 960 meters (890 to 3,150 feet), making them rarely encountered by humans.

3. Protruding Jaw: Their most distinctive feature is their long, flat snout, which houses an extendable jaw filled with sharp, fang-like teeth.

4. Electrosensory Hunter: They possess ampullae of Lorenzini, sensory organs that allow them to detect the faint electric fields emitted by other animals, aiding in locating prey in the darkness of the deep sea.

5. Pinkish Hue: Goblin sharks have a distinctive pinkish-gray coloration, which is thought to be due to the visibility of blood vessels through their translucent skin.

6. Slow-Moving Predators: They are not known for their speed or agility, but rather their ambush predation strategy, lying in wait on the seafloor before lunging at unsuspecting prey.

7. Mysterious Reproduction: Little is known about their reproductive behaviour, but they are believed to be ovoviviparous, meaning their eggs hatch within the female's body before live birth.

8. Global Distribution: While rare, goblin sharks have been found in oceans worldwide, including the Pacific, Atlantic, and Indian Oceans.

9. Unknown Lifespan: Their lifespan is still a mystery, but scientists speculate that they may live for several decades, given their slow growth and reproductive rates.

10. Research Challenges: Due to their deep-sea habitat and elusive nature, studying goblin sharks poses challenges, leaving many questions about their biology and behaviour unanswered.

Vampire Squid

1. Not a True Squid: Despite its name, the vampire squid is not a true squid but rather a unique cephalopod species classified in its own order, Vampyromorphida.

2. Relic of the Deep: It is considered a living fossil, with its lineage dating back over 300 million years, offering a glimpse into the ancient history of cephalopods.

3. Bioluminescent Master: Its body is covered in photophores (light-producing organs), allowing it to create mesmerising displays of light to deter predators and attract prey.

4. Pineapple Pose: When threatened, the vampire squid can invert its arms and web, forming a defensive "pineapple pose" that exposes spiky projections, making it appear larger and more intimidating.

5. Glow-in-the-Dark Mucus: It can eject bioluminescent mucus from its arm tips, creating a distracting cloud of light to confuse and deter attackers.

6. Low-Oxygen Specialist: Vampire squids thrive in the oxygen minimum zone, a region of the ocean with extremely low oxygen levels, where few other animals can survive.

7. Detritivore Diner: Unlike most cephalopods that hunt live prey, the vampire squid feeds primarily on marine snow, a shower of organic detritus falling from the surface.

8. Retractable Sensory Filaments: It has two long, retractile filaments that extend beyond its arms, acting as sensory organs to detect food particles and chemical cues in the water.

9. Deep-Sea Drifter: The vampire squid is a weak swimmer, relying on its gelatinous body and large fins to passively drift through the water column.

10. Cryptic Camouflage: Its dark red coloration provides excellent camouflage in the dim light of the deep sea, making it virtually invisible to predators and prey alike.

Dumbo Octopus

1. Deepest Dwelling Octopus: Dumbo octopuses hold the record for living at the deepest depths known for any octopus species, inhabiting the abyssal zone, typically at depths of 3,000 to 4,000 meters (9,800 to 13,100 feet).

2. Ear-like Fins: Their most distinctive feature is their large, ear-like fins, resembling Dumbo the elephant, which they flap to propel themselves through the water.

3. Soft and Gelatinous: Dumbo octopuses have soft, jelly-like bodies adapted to withstand the immense pressure of the deep sea, allowing them to maintain buoyancy without a hard internal or external shell.

4. No Ink Sac: Unlike most octopuses, they lack ink sacs as they rarely encounter predators in their deep-sea habitat.

5. Variety in Species: The dumbo octopus is not a single species, but rather a genus with over 15 known species, each varying in size, shape, and colour.

6. Unique Feeding Strategy: Instead of tentacles, they use their arms to create a web-like structure, trapping prey like copepods, isopods, and amphipods, and then engulfing them whole.

7. Bioluminescence: Some species of dumbo octopuses have bioluminescent organs on their suckers, which may be used for attracting prey or communicating with others.

8. Rare Encounters: Due to their deep-sea habitat, encounters with dumbo octopuses are rare, and much of their behaviour and life cycle remains a mystery.

9. No Breeding Season: They are thought to breed year-round, with females carrying eggs in various stages of development simultaneously.

10. Unexplored Territory: Studying dumbo octopuses is challenging due to their deep-sea environment, but scientists continue to explore their unique adaptations and behaviours using remotely operated vehicles (ROVs).

Sea Angel

1. Not an Angel, But a Sea Slug: Despite their angelic appearance, sea angels are a type of sea slug belonging to the group of marine gastropods called pteropods.

2. Swimming Snails: They have evolved "wings" (parapodia) from their muscular foot, allowing them to flutter gracefully through the water column like miniature angels.

3. Transparent Bodies: Sea angels are mostly transparent, making their internal organs, including their bright orange digestive system, visible.

4. Carnivorous Hunters: They are specialised predators, feeding exclusively on sea butterflies (another type of pteropod) using tentacles armed with tiny hooks and a radula (a toothed tongue-like structure).

5. Polar Dwellers: While found in oceans worldwide, the largest species of sea angels are concentrated in polar regions, where they play a crucial role in the food web.

6. Hermaphroditic Nature: Sea angels are hermaphrodites, possessing both male and female reproductive organs, and can mate with any other mature individual they encounter.

7. Mating Rituals: Their mating involves elaborate dances and the exchange of sperm packets called spermatophores.

8. Gelatinous Defences: Some species produce a chemical deterrent to protect themselves from predators like fish and jellyfish.

9. Miniature Marvels: Sea angels are typically small, with the largest species (Clione limacina) reaching a maximum length of only 5 centimetres (2 inches).

10. Ocean Acidification Threat: As the ocean becomes more acidic due to climate change, sea angels, like other shelled creatures, face challenges as their delicate shells become vulnerable to dissolution.

Sea Pig

1. Not a Pig, But a Sea Cucumber: Despite their name, sea pigs are not pigs at all. They are a type of sea cucumber belonging to the family Elpidiidae.

2. Deep-Sea Dwellers: Sea pigs inhabit the abyssal plains, the deepest parts of the ocean, typically found at depths of over 1,000 meters (3,300 feet).

3. Walking on Stilts: They have elongated tube feet, resembling stilts, that they use to "walk" along the soft, muddy seafloor.

4. Vacuum Cleaners of the Deep: Sea pigs are deposit feeders, using their tube feet to sift through sediment and extract organic matter, playing a crucial role in nutrient recycling in the deep sea.

5. Hitchhikers and Hosts: Juvenile king crabs have been observed "hitchhiking" on sea pigs, possibly as a means of protection or dispersal.

6. Defence Mechanism: When threatened, sea pigs can expel their internal organs, including their digestive and respiratory systems, as a distraction to deter predators.

7. Gelatinous Bodies: They have soft, translucent bodies filled with fluid, allowing them to withstand the immense pressure of the deep sea.

8. Diverse Diet: Sea pigs primarily consume organic matter found in the sediment, but they are opportunistic feeders and have been observed scavenging on whale carcasses.

9. Global Distribution: They are found in all major oceans, indicating their adaptability to a wide range of deep-sea environments.

10. Scientific Curiosity: Sea pigs remain relatively mysterious creatures, and scientists are still learning about their behaviour, life cycle, and ecological significance in the deep-sea ecosystem.

Barreleye Fish

1. Transparent Head: The barreleye fish (Macropinna microstoma) has a transparent, fluid-filled dome on its head, through which its tubular eyes can see.

2. Rotatable Eyes: The barreleye's eyes can rotate within its head, allowing it to look up to spot prey above or directly forward to focus on what it's eating.

3. Green Eyes for Filtering: The bright green pigment in its eyes filters out sunlight and helps it detect bioluminescence, the light emitted by other deep-sea creatures.

4. Small Mouth, Big Appetite: Despite its small mouth, the barreleye fish can swallow relatively large prey, such as siphonophores (jelly-like creatures).

5. Deep-Sea Dweller: It inhabits the twilight zone of the ocean, around 600-800 meters (2,000-2,600 feet) deep, where sunlight is scarce.

6. Stealthy Hunter: The barreleye's transparent head and upward-facing eyes help it ambush prey from below, remaining unseen while looking for food.

7. Rare Sightings: Barreleye fish are rarely encountered due to their deep-sea habitat, making them a fascinating and mysterious species.

8. Lack of Swim Bladder: Unlike many fish, barreleye fish lack a swim bladder, an organ that helps with buoyancy. Instead, they rely on their gelatinous head and flat fins to remain stable in the water.

9. Unknown Lifespan: Little is known about their lifespan or reproductive behaviour due to limited observations in their natural environment.

10. Research Challenges: The delicate nature of their transparent head makes them difficult to study, but advances in remotely operated vehicles (ROVs) are shedding new light on these enigmatic creatures.

Yeti Crab

1. Not a True Crab: The yeti crab, or Kiwa hirsuta, is not a true crab but belongs to a separate infraorder of crustaceans called Anomura. This group also includes hermit crabs and squat lobsters.

2. Hairy Appearance: Yeti crabs are named for their hairy appearance, caused by setae (stiff bristles) covering their bodies and claws. These bristles resemble fur.

3. Blind: Yeti crabs do not have eyes and are believed to rely on their setae for sensing chemicals and vibrations in their environment.

4. Deep-Sea Dwellers: Yeti crabs live near hydrothermal vents in the deep ocean, at depths of over 2,000 meters. These vents release hot, mineral-rich fluids that create unique ecosystems.

5. Farming Bacteria: Yeti crabs "farm" bacteria on their setae. They wave their claws in the water near the vents to promote bacterial growth. The bacteria serve as their primary food source.

6. New Family of Crabs: The discovery of the yeti crab in 2005 led to the establishment of a new family of crabs, Kiwaidae, due to its unique characteristics and evolutionary lineage.

7. Small Size: Yeti crabs are relatively small, with an average body length of about 15 centimetres (6 inches).

8. Extremely Dense Populations: Yeti crabs are often found in extremely dense clusters around hydrothermal vents, with hundreds of individuals per square meter.

9. Vulnerable Habitat: The survival of yeti crabs is closely linked to the presence of hydrothermal vents. Changes in vent activity could significantly impact their populations.

10. More Species Discovered: Since the initial discovery of Kiwa hirsuta, several other species of yeti crabs have been found in different parts of the world's oceans. This suggests a greater diversity of yeti crab species than previously thought.

Flamingo Tongue Snail

1. Not a Tongue, But a Mantle: The "flamingo tongue" is not actually a tongue, but a colourful mantle, a fleshy flap of tissue that covers the snail's body and shell.

2. Colour Stealing Thief: The snail's vibrant colours are not its own but come from the pigments of the soft corals it eats. It incorporates these pigments into its mantle for protection and camouflage.

3. Toxic Taste: By consuming toxic soft corals, the flamingo tongue snail becomes poisonous to predators, deterring them with its bright warning colours.

4. Coral Connoisseur: It feeds exclusively on specific types of soft corals, using its radula (a tongue-like structure with rows of tiny teeth) to scrape off the coral's tissue.

5. Caribbean Cruiser: Flamingo tongue snails are found in the tropical waters of the Caribbean Sea, the Gulf of Mexico, and the western Atlantic Ocean.

6. Limited Lifespan: These snails typically live for about a year, during which they undergo several colour changes as they grow and change their diet.

7. Shell Game: The snail's actual shell is white or cream-coloured, hidden beneath the brightly coloured mantle. It only becomes visible when the snail retracts into its shell for protection.

8. Symbiotic Relationship: Some soft corals benefit from the flamingo tongue snail's feeding habits, as it helps control the growth of certain coral species, preventing them from overgrowing and harming the reef.

9. Environmental Indicator: The presence of flamingo tongue snails can indicate the health of coral reefs, as they are sensitive to changes in water quality and coral abundance.

10. Threatened Beauty: Over harvesting for the aquarium trade and habitat destruction pose threats to flamingo tongue snail populations, highlighting the importance of responsible tourism and conservation efforts.

Bobbit Worm

1. Ambush Predator: The bobbit worm is a fearsome ambush predator found in warm ocean waters. It buries most of its body in the sand, leaving only its mouthparts exposed, to surprise unsuspecting prey.

2. Impressive Size: Bobbit worms can reach incredible lengths, with some specimens reported to grow up to 10 feet long. However, average lengths are usually between 2 to 4 feet.

3. Powerful Jaws: Their jaws are wider than their body and can snap shut with incredible speed and force, allowing them to capture and slice prey in half, including fish, squid, and other worms.

4. Sharp Bristles: Bobbit worms have sharp bristles lining their bodies, which help them anchor in their burrows and provide traction when attacking prey.

5. Venomous Bite: They inject venom into their prey through their bite, paralysing or killing them before dragging them into their burrows for consumption.

6. Nocturnal Hunters: Bobbit worms are primarily nocturnal hunters, relying on their five antennae to sense movement and vibrations in the water to locate potential meals.

7. Longevity: These worms are believed to have a long lifespan, with some individuals potentially living for decades.

8. Mucus-Lined Burrows: They create mucus-lined burrows in the ocean floor, which provide stability and protection from predators.

9. Aquarium Menace: Bobbit worms have been known to wreak havoc in aquariums, as they can easily hide in the substrate and prey on unsuspecting fish.

10. Ancient Origins: Fossil evidence suggests that bobbit worms have been around for at least 20 million years, highlighting their successful evolutionary adaptations.

Christmas Tree Worm

1. Festive Appearance: Christmas tree worms are named for their colourful, spiral-shaped plumes that resemble miniature Christmas trees. These plumes come in various vibrant colours like red, orange, yellow, blue, and white.

2. Tube-Dwelling Worms: They are tube-dwelling polychaete worms, meaning they live inside tubes they build in coral reefs. These tubes provide protection and support.

3. Filter Feeders: Their "Christmas trees" are specialised feeding structures. They use these to filter plankton and other tiny organisms from the water, which are then transported to their mouths.

4. Sensitive to Light and Movement: Christmas tree worms are highly sensitive to changes in light and movement. They quickly retract their plumes into their tubes when they sense a threat, making them difficult to spot.

5. Long Lifespan: Despite their small size, Christmas tree worms can live for up to 40 years in their coral homes.

6. Symbiotic Relationship with Coral: They have a symbiotic relationship with coral reefs. They provide the coral with nutrients, and the coral offers them a safe place to live.

7. Worldwide Distribution: Christmas tree worms can be found in tropical and subtropical waters worldwide, typically inhabiting shallow coral reefs.

8. Diverse Species: There are over 100 different species of Christmas tree worms, each with unique colour patterns and variations in their plumes.

9. Indicator Species: Their presence and health can serve as indicators of the overall health of coral reefs, as they are sensitive to environmental changes.

10. Important for Reef Ecosystems: Christmas tree worms play a crucial role in maintaining the balance of coral reef ecosystems by filtering the water and contributing to nutrient cycling.

Pompeii Worm

1. Extremophile Champion: Pompeii worms (Alvinella pompejana) are one of the most heat-tolerant animals on Earth, thriving in the superheated waters of deep-sea hydrothermal vents.

2. Bacterial Armour: They are covered in a thick, fleece-like layer of bacteria, which helps insulate them from the extreme temperatures and may provide them with nutrients.

3. Temperature Tolerance: Pompeii worms can withstand temperatures as high as 80°C (176°F) on their back ends, while their heads experience cooler temperatures of around 22°C (72°F).

4. Tube-Dwelling Worms: They build protective tubes from minerals in the vent fluids, providing shelter and further insulation from the harsh environment.

5. Deep-Sea Oases: Pompeii worms are keystone species in hydrothermal vent ecosystems, forming the base of a unique food web that supports a variety of other organisms.

6. Red-Headed Wonders: They have bright red, feathery gills that absorb oxygen and expel waste products, essential for survival in the low-oxygen environment of the vents.

7. Symbiotic Relationship: The bacteria covering Pompeii worms have a symbiotic relationship with their host, possibly providing food or detoxification services in exchange for a stable habitat.

8. Scientific Marvels: Their remarkable adaptations to extreme environments have made Pompeii worms a subject of intense scientific research, offering insights into the limits of life on Earth.

9. Limited Lifespan: Despite their resilience, Pompeii worms have a relatively short lifespan, typically living for only one to two years.

10. Due to their deep-sea habitat, Pompeii worms were only discovered in the 1980s, highlighting the vastness and mystery of the ocean depths and the extraordinary life forms.

Water Bear

1. Microscopic Size: Water bears, also known as tardigrades, are microscopic animals typically measuring less than 1 millimetre in length. They are barely visible to the naked eye.

2. Eight Legs: They have eight legs, each tipped with four to eight claws or digits, giving them a lumbering walk resembling a bear's gait.

3. Extreme Survivalists: Water bears are renowned for their extreme resilience and ability to survive in harsh environments that would kill most other life forms.

4. Cryptobiosis: They can enter a state of suspended animation called cryptobiosis when faced with extreme conditions like dehydration, freezing, or radiation. Their metabolism slows down to almost zero, and they can remain in this state for decades.

5. Space Survivors: Tardigrades have even survived exposure to the vacuum of space and harmful radiation, making them the first known animal to do so.

6. Diverse Habitats: They can be found in a variety of habitats worldwide, including moss, lichen, soil, freshwater, and even the ocean depths.

7. Variety of Diets: Water bears have diverse diets. Some are herbivores, feeding on plant cells, while others are carnivores or omnivores, consuming bacteria, algae, and even other tardigrades.

8. Unique Body Plan: Their bodies have a unique segmented structure with a flexible cuticle that allows them to shrink and expand.

9. Molting: Like many other invertebrates, water bears molt their outer cuticle as they grow.

10. Model Organisms: Due to their incredible resilience and adaptability, water bears are used as model organisms in scientific research to study stress tolerance, survival mechanisms, and even potential applications in medicine and biotechnology.

Comb Jelly

1. Not a Jellyfish: Though they share a similar gelatinous appearance, comb jellies (Ctenophora) are not jellyfish. They belong to their own distinct phylum, separate from Cnidaria (which includes jellyfish).

2. Rainbow Warriors: Comb jellies are known for their shimmering iridescence, caused by the refraction of light on their eight rows of comb-like plates (ctenes) used for swimming.

3. Bioluminescent Beauties: Many species are bioluminescent, meaning they can produce their own light. This light can be used for communication, attracting prey, or confusing predators.

4. Sticky Predators: They capture prey using specialised sticky cells called colloblasts, located on their tentacles. These cells release adhesive threads to ensnare small organisms.

5. Voracious Appetite: Comb jellies are voracious predators, feeding on a wide variety of plankton, including fish larvae, crustaceans, and even other comb jellies.

6. Diverse Body Shapes: They come in various shapes and sizes, from tiny, spherical species to long, ribbon-like forms, and even some resembling walnuts.

7. Ancient Origins: Comb jellies have a long evolutionary history, with fossils dating back over 500 million years, making them some of the oldest animals on Earth.

8. Invasive Impact: Some species, like the sea walnut (Mnemiopsis leidyi), have become invasive in certain regions, causing significant ecological disruptions due to their high predation rates.

9. Self-Fertilisation: Many comb jellies are hermaphrodites, capable of self-fertilisation, meaning they can reproduce without a mate.

10. Important Ecosystem Role: Despite their potential for invasiveness, comb jellies play crucial roles in marine ecosystems as predators and prey, contributing to nutrient cycling and energy flow in the food web.

Salp

1. Not a Jellyfish: Salps are often mistaken for jellyfish due to their translucent bodies, but they are actually tunicates, more closely related to humans than to jellyfish.

2. Jet Propulsion: Salps propel themselves by pumping water through their bodies, making them one of the most efficient jet-propelled organisms in the animal kingdom.

3. Chain Gang: Salps can form long, interconnected chains of individuals, sometimes stretching for meters. These chains move and feed together, creating a mesmerising spectacle.

4. Filter Feeders: They feed on phytoplankton, tiny marine plants, by filtering them out of the water using their internal mucous nets.

5. Rapid Growth: Salps have a remarkable growth rate, sometimes doubling their population size in a single day under favourable conditions.

6. Carbon Sink: Their feeding and excretion habits contribute to the ocean's biological pump, transporting carbon from the surface to the depths, where it is sequestered.

7. Bioluminescent Glow: Some species of salps are bioluminescent, creating a mesmerising underwater light show, especially when they form large swarms.

8. Blooms and Busts: Salp populations can undergo dramatic boom-and-bust cycles, with massive blooms followed by rapid declines, influenced by factors like food availability and predation.

9. Food Web Impact: They play a crucial role in marine food webs, serving as prey for various animals, including fish, turtles, and seabirds.

10. Climate Change Indicators: Their distribution and abundance are sensitive to changes in ocean temperature and currents, making them potential indicators of climate change impacts on marine ecosystems.

Sea Urchins

1. Sea urchins belong to the phylum Echinodermata, which also includes starfish and sea cucumbers.

2. They have a hard exoskeleton called a "test," made of calcium carbonate plates.

3. Their mouth is located on their underside, and they have a unique jaw structure called Aristotle's lantern.

4. They move using tube feet, which are small, flexible appendages filled with water.

5. Sea urchins are omnivores, primarily eating algae but also consuming other small organisms.

6. Some species can live for over 100 years.

7. They play an important role in maintaining the balance of marine ecosystems, particularly kelp forests.

8. They reproduce by releasing eggs and sperm into the water, where fertilisation occurs externally.

9. Some sea urchin species are harvested for their gonads (uni), considered a delicacy in many cultures.

10. Sea urchins have a variety of defence mechanisms, including spines, pedicellariae (pincer-like organs), and venom.

Crabs

1. Crabs have teeth in their stomachs: Crabs have a gastric mill, a grinding structure in their stomach that helps break down food using calcified teeth-like structures.

2. Crabs can survive out of water for surprising lengths of time: Some species of crabs, particularly those found in intertidal zones, have adapted to survive for hours or even days out of water.

3. Male crabs fight intense battles for mating rights: During mating season, male crabs will engage in fierce claw-to-claw combat to establish dominance and gain access to females.

4. Crabs have a special "urine" sense: Crabs have chemoreceptors on their antennae that allow them to detect chemical signals in the urine of other crabs, which helps them find mates and assess potential rivals.

5. Crabs are incredibly diverse: There are over 6,700 known species of crabs, inhabiting a wide range of marine environments from shallow coastal waters to the depths of the ocean.

6. Some crabs can swim: While most crabs are known for their sideways scuttle, certain species like the blue swimmer crab have paddle-like back legs that allow them to swim effectively.

7. Crabs can hear using their legs: Crabs have sensory hairs on their legs that detect vibrations in the water, allowing them to "hear" approaching predators or prey.

8. Crabs have a unique way of breathing: Crabs use gills to extract oxygen from the water, but unlike fish, they can also breathe through their skin as long as it remains moist.

9. Crabs are expert escape artists: Crabs have a remarkable ability to squeeze through incredibly narrow spaces thanks to their flexible joints and flattened bodies.

10. Some crabs use camouflage to avoid predators: Certain species of crabs decorate their shells with algae, sponges, or other materials to blend in with their surroundings and avoid detection by predators.

Tuna

1. Tuna are warm-blooded: Unlike most fish, tuna can maintain a body temperature higher than the surrounding water, allowing them to thrive in both cold and warm oceans.

2. Tuna are incredibly fast swimmers: Certain species of tuna, like the yellowfin and bluefin, can reach speeds of up to 43 miles per hour (70 km/h), making them some of the fastest fish in the ocean.

3. Tuna migrate vast distances: Tuna are known for their long-distance migrations, often travelling thousands of miles across oceans in search of food and breeding grounds.

4. Tuna are apex predators: Tuna occupy a high position in the marine food chain, preying on smaller fish, squid, and crustaceans.

5. Tuna come in various sizes: There are over 15 species of tuna, ranging from the relatively small skipjack tuna to the massive bluefin tuna, which can grow to over 10 feet (3 meters) long and weigh over 1,000 pounds (450 kg).

6. Tuna are valuable commercially: Tuna is a highly sought-after fish for both sport and commercial fishing, with millions of tons caught annually worldwide.

7. Tuna are overfished: Due to their popularity and high demand, several tuna species are facing overfishing concerns, with populations declining significantly in recent years.

8. Tuna are a good source of omega-3 fatty acids: Tuna is rich in omega-3 fatty acids, which are essential for human health, promoting heart health, brain function, and reducing inflammation.

9. Tuna can hold their breath: Tuna have a specialised adaptation called a rete mirabile, which allows them to extract oxygen from the water more efficiently, enabling them to hold their breath for extended periods while hunting.

10. Tuna have a unique body shape: Tuna possess a streamlined, torpedo-shaped body with a powerful tail fin, allowing them to swim efficiently and with great speed.

Stingrays

1. Stingrays are cartilaginous fish, meaning their skeletons are made of cartilage instead of bone, similar to sharks.

2. They have flat, disc-shaped bodies and long, whip-like tails often equipped with venomous barbs used for defence.

3. Stingrays are found in various marine habitats, from shallow coastal waters to deeper ocean depths.

4. They are bottom dwellers, using their flat bodies to camouflage themselves on the seafloor while hunting for prey.

5. Their diet primarily consists of crustaceans, molluscs, and small fish, which they crush with their powerful jaws.

6. Stingrays reproduce through internal fertilisation, and most species give birth to live young called "pups."

7. They have specialised organs called ampullae of Lorenzini that allow them to sense the electrical fields generated by other animals, aiding in prey detection.

8. Stingrays are not typically aggressive toward humans, but they will sting if they feel threatened or are accidentally stepped on.

9. Some species of stingrays are considered endangered due to overfishing and habitat destruction.

10. The largest stingray species is the giant oceanic manta ray, which can reach a wingspan of up to 29 feet.

Fast Fish

1. Sailfish is the Fastest: Sailfish are considered the fastest fish in the ocean, reaching speeds up to 68 mph (110 km/h) in short bursts.

2. Black Marlin's Incredible Acceleration: Black marlin can accelerate incredibly fast, reportedly reaching 80 mph (128 km/h) in just a few seconds.

3. Swordfish are Fast and Powerful: Swordfish are known for their speed and agility, reaching speeds up to 60 mph (97 km/h), aided by their sharp bill.

4. Tuna are High-Speed Predators: Some tuna species, like the yellowfin tuna, are exceptionally fast swimmers, reaching speeds of 43 mph (70 km/h) while chasing prey.

5. Mako Sharks are Agile Hunters: Shortfin mako sharks are the fastest sharks, reaching speeds up to 46 mph (74 km/h), making them formidable predators in the open ocean.

6. Wahoo are Speedy and Streamlined: Wahoo are known for their impressive acceleration and streamlined bodies, allowing them to reach speeds up to 48 mph (77 km/h).

7. Bonefish are Surprisingly Fast: Bonefish, typically found in shallow waters, are surprisingly fast swimmers, capable of reaching speeds up to 40 mph (64 km/h) in short bursts.

8. Blue Sharks are Open-Ocean Sprinters: Blue sharks are known for their endurance and speed, capable of maintaining speeds of up to 43 mph (69 km/h) over long distances.

9. Flying Fish Glide Above the Surface: While not technically swimming, flying fish can "fly" out of the water and glide for distances up to 655 feet (200 meters) at speeds of up to 35 mph (56 km/h).

10. Speed is Key for Survival: The fastest fish in the sea rely on their speed for hunting, escaping predators, and migrating vast distances across the oceans.

Sailfish

1. Fastest Fish in the Ocean: Sailfish are considered the fastest fish in the ocean, capable of reaching speeds up to 68 mph (110 km/h) in short bursts.

2. Impressive Dorsal Fin: The sailfish's most striking feature is its large dorsal fin, known as a sail, which it raises when excited or hunting.

3. Sail Used for Hunting: The sail is not just for show; sailfish use it to herd schools of smaller fish, making them easier to catch.

4. Billfish Family: Sailfish belong to the billfish family, a group of fish characterized by their elongated, pointed bills.

5. Worldwide Distribution: Sailfish are found in tropical and subtropical waters around the world, including the Atlantic, Pacific, and Indian Oceans.

6. Voracious Predators: Sailfish are apex predators, feeding on a variety of smaller fish, squid, and crustaceans.

7. Impressive Leaping Ability: Sailfish are known for their acrobatic leaps out of the water, often putting on a spectacular show for anglers and observers.

8. Popular Game Fish: Sailfish are highly sought after by sport fishermen due to their speed, strength, and fighting ability.

9. Conservation Concerns: Overfishing has led to population declines in some areas, and sailfish are now considered a vulnerable species by the International Union for Conservation of Nature (IUCN).

10. Lifespan: Sailfish have a relatively short lifespan, typically living for 4-5 years in the wild.

Black Marlin

1. The black marlin (Istiompax indica) is a large, predatory fish found in the tropical and subtropical waters of the Indian and Pacific Oceans.

2. It is one of the largest bony fish in the world, with females often exceeding 4 meters (13 feet) in length and weighing over 750 kilograms (1,650 pounds).

3. Black marlins are known for their impressive speed and strength, making them a popular game fish among anglers.

4. They have a distinctive elongated upper jaw, resembling a spear or bill, which they use to stun or injure prey.

5. Their diet primarily consists of smaller fish, squid, and octopus.

6. Black marlins are highly migratory fish, travelling long distances in search of food and suitable breeding grounds.

7. Females can release millions of eggs during spawning, which are then fertilised by the males.

8. Black marlins are considered a vulnerable species due to overfishing and habitat degradation.

9. They are an apex predator, playing a crucial role in maintaining the balance of marine ecosystems.

10. Their sleek, streamlined bodies and powerful tails make them one of the fastest fish in the ocean, capable of reaching speeds up to 80 kilometers per hour (50 miles per hour).

10 Big

1. Blue Whale (Largest Animal Ever): The blue whale is the largest animal to have ever existed, even bigger than the largest dinosaurs. Its heart is the size of a small car.

2. Lion's Mane Jellyfish (Longest Animal): With tentacles that can reach over 120 feet long, the lion's mane jellyfish is the longest known animal on Earth.

3. Colossal Squid (Largest Invertebrate): This deep-sea dweller has the largest eyes in the animal kingdom, about the size of dinner plates.

4. Whale Shark (Largest Fish): Despite its name, the whale shark is a fish, not a whale. It's a filter feeder, primarily consuming plankton.

5. Giant Manta Ray (Largest Ray): This graceful creature has a wingspan of up to 29 feet and is known for its intelligence and playful behaviour.

6. Giant Squid (Largest Cephalopod): With enormous tentacles and a powerful beak, the giant squid is a fearsome predator of the deep sea.

7. Giant Oarfish (Longest Bony Fish): This elusive fish can grow to over 50 feet long and is often mistaken for a sea serpent due to its elongated body.

8. Basking Shark (Second-Largest Fish): This gentle giant is another filter feeder, primarily consuming plankton.

9. Ocean Sunfish (Heaviest Bony Fish): This strange-looking fish can weigh up to 5,000 pounds and is known for its unique shape and behaviour.

10. Humpback Whale (Largest Seasonal Migrator): Humpback whales make some of the longest migrations of any mammal, travelling thousands of miles between feeding and breeding grounds.

10 Small

1. Marine Viruses: These microscopic entities are the smallest biological forms in the ocean, playing crucial roles in marine ecosystems and nutrient cycles.

2. Marine Bacteria: Slightly larger than viruses, bacteria are incredibly abundant in the ocean, contributing to various ecological processes and even forming symbiotic relationships with other marine organisms.

3. Zooplankton: This diverse group includes tiny crustaceans, jellyfish, and other microscopic animals that form the base of the marine food web, serving as a primary food source for many larger creatures.

4. Irukandji Jellyfish: Found in tropical waters, this tiny jellyfish is one of the most venomous creatures on Earth, despite its size of only about a cubic centimetre.

5. Pygmy Seahorse: Measuring less than an inch long, the pygmy seahorse is a master of camouflage, blending seamlessly with its coral habitat.

6. Nudibranchs: These colourful sea slugs come in a variety of shapes and sizes, with some species measuring less than a centimetre long.

7. Dwarf Lanternshark: This deep-sea shark is the smallest shark species, growing to only about 8 inches long.

8. Sexy Shrimp: Also known as the squat shrimp, this tiny crustacean is known for its bright colours and "dancing" movements.

9. Octopus Wolfi: This miniature octopus is one of the smallest cephalopods, measuring less than an inch long.

10. Paedocypris: This genus of fish includes some of the smallest known vertebrates, with some species reaching only 7.9 mm in length.

10 Colourful

1. Mandarin fish: This small, psychedelic fish is often considered the most colourful fish in the world, with a vibrant pattern of blue, orange, yellow, and green.

2. Nudibranchs: These sea slugs come in a dazzling array of colours and patterns, often resembling jewels or flowers.

3. Peacock Mantis Shrimp: This crustacean is not only one of the most colourful, but also one of the most aggressive creatures in the sea, with its vibrant hues serving as a warning to potential rivals.

4. Clown fish: Made famous by the movie Finding Nemo, clown fish are known for their bright orange and white stripes, contrasted with black fins.

5. Parrot fish: These fish are named for their beak-like mouths, which they use to scrape algae off coral reefs. They come in a variety of colours, including blue, green, orange, and pink.

6. Sea Anemones: While not technically fish, these vibrant creatures add a burst of colour to coral reefs, with their tentacles coming in shades of pink, purple, orange, and red.

7. Christmas Tree Worms: These marine worms live in colourful tubes that resemble Christmas trees, with their feathery appendages used for feeding and respiration.

8. Blue-Ringed Octopus: This small octopus may look harmless, but its vibrant blue rings are a warning sign of its deadly venom.

9. Lionfish: These invasive fish are known for their beautiful, fan-like fins, which are striped with venomous spines.

10. Regal Angelfish: This stunning fish is found in the Indo-Pacific and is known for its bright blue and yellow stripes, accented with black and white markings.

10 Most deadly

1. Box Jellyfish: These transparent creatures have venom powerful enough to kill a human within minutes.

2. Blue-Ringed Octopus: Don't be fooled by their small size and beautiful blue rings; their venom is neurotoxic and can cause respiratory failure.

3. Stonefish: Masters of camouflage, these bottom-dwelling fish have venomous spines that can cause excruciating pain and even death.

4. Puffer fish: While a delicacy in some cultures, puffer fish contain tetrodotoxin, a potent neurotoxin that can be lethal if not prepared properly.

5. Cone Snail: These beautiful snails pack a deadly harpoon-like tooth filled with venom that can paralyse and kill prey.

6. Sea Snakes: Highly venomous, sea snakes have potent neurotoxins that can cause paralysis and respiratory failure.

7. Lionfish: These invasive species have venomous spines that can cause painful stings and pose a threat to native ecosystems.

8. Stingrays: While not typically aggressive, stingrays have venomous barbs on their tails that can inflict serious wounds if stepped on.

9. Portuguese Man o' War: This colony of organisms resembles a jellyfish and has long tentacles with stinging cells that can cause severe pain and allergic reactions.

10. Marbled Cone Snail: This snail's venom is a complex cocktail of toxins that can cause paralysis, respiratory failure, and even death.

10 Best hunters

1. Orca (Killer Whale): Orcas are apex predators with sophisticated hunting strategies, working together to take down large prey like seals, sea lions, and even other whales.

2. Great White Shark: This iconic predator is known for its powerful jaws and sharp teeth, using stealth and surprise to ambush seals, sea lions, and other marine mammals.

3. Humboldt Squid: These aggressive cephalopods hunt in packs, using their sharp beaks and powerful tentacles to capture fish, squid, and crustaceans.

4. Sailfish: The fastest fish in the ocean, sailfish use their speed and agility to chase down smaller fish, stunning them with their bills before devouring them.

5. Bottlenose Dolphin: These intelligent marine mammals use echolocation to locate prey and work together to herd fish into tight balls for easier capture.

6. Giant Trevally: This powerful fish is an opportunistic predator, ambushing prey in reefs and using its strong jaws to crush shells and exoskeletons.

7. Sea Otter: These adorable creatures are surprisingly skilled hunters, using rocks to crack open sea urchins and other shellfish.

8. Barracuda: These sleek fish are ambush predators, lurking in wait for unsuspecting prey before striking with lightning speed and sharp teeth.

9. Anglerfish: This deep-sea dweller uses a bioluminescent lure to attract prey, then snaps them up with its massive jaws.

10. Remora: While not a traditional predator, remoras have a unique hunting strategy, attaching themselves to larger animals like sharks and whales to scavenge scraps and leftover prey.

10 Ocean Facts

1. The oceans cover more than 70 percent of the Earth's surface, making it the largest habitat on our planet.

2. The average depth of the ocean is about 2.3 miles (3.7 kilometers).

3. The Mariana Trench is the deepest part of the ocean, reaching a depth of about 7 miles (11 kilometers). The deep ocean remains largely unexplored, with many unique and bizarre creatures yet to be discovered.

4. Scientists estimate that 91% of ocean species have yet to be classified.

5. The longest mountain range on Earth is underwater. The Mid-Ocean Ridge stretches for about 40,390 miles (65,000 km).

6. The oceans produce about 70% of the oxygen we breathe, mainly through the phytoplankton that live there.

7. Underwater Mountains: The longest mountain range on Earth, the Mid-Ocean Ridge, is located underwater and stretches for about 40,390 miles (65,000 kilometres)

8. Sunlight can only penetrate the ocean up to a depth of about 656 feet (200 meters), leaving the rest in perpetual darkness.

9. Hydrothermal vents, underwater geysers, support unique ecosystems that thrive in extreme heat and pressure.

10. The Great Garbage Patch, located in the Pacific Ocean, is an area of marine debris concentration formed by ocean currents. Human activities, such as pollution, overfishing, and climate change, are threatening the health of the oceans and the marine life they support.

10 Of the deepest

1. Mariana Trench: Located in the western Pacific Ocean, the Mariana Trench is the deepest known part of the Earth's oceans and the deepest location on Earth's surface. The Challenger Deep within the trench is estimated to be 10,984 meters (36,037 feet) deep.

2. Tonga Trench: Situated in the South Pacific Ocean, the Tonga Trench reaches a depth of 10,882 meters (35,702 feet). It's known for its active tectonic plate activity.

3. Philippine Trench: Also known as the Mindanao Trench, it's located in the western Pacific Ocean and has a maximum depth of 10,540 meters (34,580 feet).

4. Kuril-Kamchatka Trench: This trench in the northwest Pacific Ocean has a maximum depth of 10,500 meters (34,449 feet) and is associated with volcanic activity.

5. Kermadec Trench: Found in the South Pacific Ocean, the Kermadec Trench reaches a depth of 10,047 meters (32,963 feet) and is home to unique deep-sea ecosystems.

6. Izu-Ogasawara Trench: Located south of Japan in the western Pacific Ocean, this trench has a maximum depth of 9,780 meters (32,087 feet).

7. Japan Trench: Also known as the Izu-Bonin Trench, it runs along the eastern coast of Japan and reaches depths of 9,000 meters (29,528 feet).

8. Puerto Rico Trench: This trench in the Atlantic Ocean has a maximum depth of 8,376 meters (27,480 feet) and is the deepest point in the Atlantic.

9. Peru-Chile Trench: Also known as the Atacama Trench, it runs along the western coast of South America and reaches depths of 8,065 meters (26,460 feet).

10. Diamantina Trench: Located in the southeastern Indian Ocean, this trench has a maximum depth of 8,047 meters (26,401 feet).

10 of the Coldest Seas

1. The Southern Ocean: Surrounding Antarctica, this ocean is known for its frigid temperatures, with average surface water temperatures hovering around -2 to 10 °C (28 to 50 °F).

2. Arctic Ocean: The Arctic Ocean, located around the North Pole, is another incredibly cold body of water, with average temperatures below freezing for much of the year.

3. The Weddell Sea: This southernmost sea of the Atlantic Ocean is covered in ice for most of the year, making it one of the coldest and most inhospitable marine environments on Earth.

4. The Ross Sea: Another frigid expanse of the Southern Ocean, the Ross Sea is home to a vast ice shelf and numerous glaciers, contributing to its cold temperatures.

5. The Labrador Sea: This North Atlantic sea experiences extremely cold winters, with water temperatures often dipping below freezing due to the influence of the Labrador Current.

6. The Greenland Sea: Located between Greenland and Svalbard, this sea is known for its icy waters, with temperatures rarely rising above freezing even in summer.

7. The Bering Sea: This Pacific Ocean sea, located between Alaska and Russia, is known for its harsh conditions, with cold temperatures and frequent storms.

8. The Sea of Okhotsk: This sea, located between Russia and Japan, experiences long, cold winters with extensive sea ice formation.

9. The Norwegian Sea: This North Atlantic sea is home to the Norwegian Current, a warm current that moderates temperatures somewhat, but it still experiences cold winters with occasional sea ice.

10. The Baltic Sea: While not as cold as some other seas on this list, the Baltic Sea experiences cold winters and can freeze over in some areas.

10 of the Hottest Seas

1. Persian Gulf: Known for its extremely high water temperatures, especially during the summer months, where it can reach up to 90°F (32°C).

2. Red Sea: This narrow sea is surrounded by desert, leading to high evaporation rates and warm water temperatures, often exceeding 86°F (30°C).

3. Indian Ocean: Especially in the areas around the equator and near Southeast Asia, the Indian Ocean experiences consistently warm temperatures, averaging between 77-86°F (25-30°C).

4. Caribbean Sea: This popular tourist destination boasts warm, clear waters throughout the year, with temperatures ranging from 75-85°F (24-29°C).

5. Gulf of Mexico: Similar to the Caribbean, the Gulf of Mexico is known for its warm waters, particularly during the summer months, where temperatures can reach the mid-80s°F (around 29°C).

6. Coral Sea: Located off the coast of Australia, the Coral Sea is home to the Great Barrier Reef and experiences warm temperatures year-round, typically between 75-84°F (24-29°C).

7. South China Sea: This large, semi-enclosed sea is influenced by tropical climates and experiences warm temperatures, with averages ranging from 77-86°F (25-30°C).

8. Gulf of Thailand: A popular tourist destination, the Gulf of Thailand boasts consistently warm waters, with temperatures averaging between 82-86°F (28-30°C).

9. Andaman Sea: Located between the Indian Ocean and the Andaman Islands, this sea is known for its crystal-clear waters and warm temperatures, ranging from 80-86°F (27-30°C).

10. Sea of Cortez (Gulf of California): This narrow sea between Baja California and mainland Mexico experiences warm temperatures, particularly in the southern regions, where it can reach the mid-80s°F (around 29°C).

10 of the biggest Coral Reefs

1. Great Barrier Reef (Australia): The largest coral reef system in the world, stretching over 2,300 kilometres (1,400 miles) and comprising thousands of individual reefs.

2. Mesoamerican Barrier Reef System (Caribbean Sea): The second-largest coral reef system, extending along the coasts of Mexico, Belize, Guatemala, and Honduras.

3. New Caledonia Barrier Reef (New Caledonia): The second-longest double barrier reef in the world, known for its diverse marine life and unique coral formations.

4. Red Sea Coral Reef (Red Sea): A resilient reef system stretching over 2,000 kilometres (1,240 miles) along the coasts of Egypt, Saudi Arabia, and Sudan.

5. Andros Barrier Reef (Bahamas): The third-largest barrier reef in the world, located off the coast of Andros Island and known for its deep water sponges and diverse fish populations.

6. Florida Reef Tract (United States): The only living coral barrier reef in the continental United States, extending from the Florida Keys to the Dry Tortugas.

7. Saya de Malha Bank (Indian Ocean): A submerged atoll and the largest submerged bank in the world, supporting a vast and diverse coral ecosystem.

8. Great Chagos Bank (Indian Ocean): The largest atoll structure in the world, located in the Chagos Archipelago and home to a variety of coral species.

9. Reed Bank (South China Sea): A large submerged atoll in the disputed Spratly Islands, known for its rich marine biodiversity and extensive coral reefs.

10. Apo Reef (Philippines): The second-largest contiguous coral reef in the world, located in the Mindoro Strait and known for its diverse marine life, including sharks, manta rays, and sea turtles.

Great Barrier Reef

1. The Great Barrier Reef is the world's largest coral reef system composed of over 2,900 individual reefs and 900 islands stretching for over 2,300 kilometres (1,400 miles) over an area of approximately 344,400 square kilometres (133,000 sq mi).

2. The Great Barrier Reef can be seen from outer space and is the world's biggest single structure made by living organisms.

3. The Great Barrier Reef supports a wide diversity of life, including more than 1,500 species of fish, 411 types of hard coral, one-third of the world's soft corals, 134 species of sharks and rays, six of the world's seven species of threatened marine turtles and more than 30 species of marine mammals.

4. The Great Barrier Reef is a crucial habitat for the dugong, a large marine mammal that is listed as vulnerable to extinction.

5. The reef is home to 215 species of birds (including 22 species of seabirds and 32 species of shorebirds) that visit the reef or nest or roost on the islands.

6. Indigenous Australians have been living in harmony with the Great Barrier Reef for at least 60,000 years.

7. The reef generates more than A$6 billion for the Australian economy each year through tourism and fishing.

8. Climate change poses a serious threat to the Great Barrier Reef. Rising sea temperatures and ocean acidification are causing widespread coral bleaching and mortality.

9. The Great Barrier Reef Marine Park Authority is responsible for managing and protecting the Great Barrier Reef Marine Park.

10. The Great Barrier Reef is a UNESCO World Heritage Site, recognised for its outstanding universal value.

Mesoamerican Barrier Reef System (MBRS)

1. The Mesoamerican Barrier Reef System (MBRS) is the second-largest barrier reef in the world, spanning over 1,000 kilometres (620 miles) along the coasts of Mexico, Belize, Guatemala, and Honduras.

2. This reef system is home to an incredible diversity of marine life, with over 500 species of fish, 65 species of stony coral, 350 species of mollusc, and various species of sea turtles, manatees, and dolphins.

3. The MBRS plays a critical role in protecting coastal communities from storms and erosion, acting as a natural buffer against the waves and currents.

4. The Belize Barrier Reef, a significant part of the MBRS, is a UNESCO World Heritage Site, recognised for its outstanding universal value.

5. The Great Blue Hole, a giant marine sinkhole off the coast of Belize, is a world-renowned dive site and part of the MBRS.

6. The MBRS faces numerous threats, including climate change, pollution, overfishing, and coastal development.

7. Conservation efforts are underway to protect the MBRS, involving collaboration between governments, NGOs, and local communities.

8. The MBRS is a crucial source of income for local communities through tourism and fishing.

9. The reef system supports various ecosystems, including mangroves, seagrass beds, and lagoons, each contributing to its biodiversity.

10. The Mesoamerican Reef Fund (MAR Fund) is a key organisation dedicated to conserving the MBRS and promoting sustainable use of its resources.

New Caledonia Reef

1. The New Caledonia Barrier Reef is the longest continuous barrier reef in the world, stretching over 1,600 kilometres (990 miles).

2. It encircles Grande Terre, New Caledonia's main island, as well as the Île des Pins and several smaller islands.

3. The reef encloses a lagoon of 24,000 square kilometres (9,300 square miles), making it one of the largest lagoons in the world.

4. This dual barrier reef system is considered the third-largest in the world, after the Great Barrier Reef in Australia and the Mesoamerican Barrier Reef.

5. New Caledonia's reef system boasts exceptional biodiversity, hosting over 9,300 marine species, including many that are endemic to the region.

6. The reef is home to diverse coral species, with over 350 recorded species of hard coral.

7. Six of New Caledonia's lagoons and coral reefs have been designated as UNESCO World Heritage Sites, recognising their outstanding universal value.

8. The reef plays a crucial role in protecting the coastline from erosion and storm damage.

9. New Caledonia's reefs and lagoons offer exceptional opportunities for snorkeling, diving, and other water activities, attracting tourists from around the world.

10. Efforts are underway to conserve and protect New Caledonia's unique reef system, including the establishment of marine protected areas and sustainable tourism practices.

Red Sea Coral reef

1. Vibrant Coral Diversity: The Red Sea is home to over 200 species of hard and soft corals, creating a vibrant underwater landscape with diverse formations and colours.

2. Endemic Species: The Red Sea boasts a high level of endemism, meaning many species found here are not found anywhere else in the world. This includes unique coral species and fish species like the Red Sea anemonefish.

3. Ancient Reefs: Some of the coral reefs in the Red Sea are estimated to be over 5,000 years old, making them some of the oldest living coral formations on Earth.

4. High Salinity: The Red Sea is known for its high salinity, which creates a unique environment for coral growth and supports the survival of certain species that are adapted to these conditions.

5. Thriving Fish Populations: The coral reefs of the Red Sea support a rich diversity of fish species, with over 1,200 species recorded, including colourful butterfly fish, angelfish, and parrot fish.

6. Shark Haven: The Red Sea is home to over 40 species of sharks, including reef sharks, hammerheads, and whale sharks, attracting divers and researchers from around the world.

7. Resilience to Climate Change: While coral reefs globally are threatened by climate change, the Red Sea's corals have shown surprising resilience to rising temperatures, giving hope for their survival in the face of environmental challenges.

8. Important Ecosystem Services: The coral reefs of the Red Sea provide essential ecosystem services, such as protecting coastlines from erosion, supporting fisheries, and contributing to the local economy through tourism.

9. World-Class Dive Destination: The Red Sea is renowned as a premier diving destination, offering unparalleled opportunities to explore its vibrant coral reefs and diverse marine life.

10. Conservation Efforts: Numerous conservation initiatives are underway in the Red Sea to protect its coral reefs, including the establishment of marine protected areas, efforts to reduce pollution, and initiatives to promote sustainable tourism practices.

Andros Barrier Reef

1. Third-Largest Barrier Reef: The Andros Barrier Reef is the third-largest barrier reef in the world, stretching for over 124 miles (200 kilometres) along the eastern coast of Andros Island in the Bahamas.

2. Biodiversity Hotspot: The reef is a biodiversity hotspot, home to a vast array of marine life, including over 164 species of fish and 50 species of coral.

3. Deep Water Trench: The reef runs parallel to the Tongue of the Ocean, a deep water trench that plunges to depths of over 6,000 feet (1,800 meters). This unique geography creates a diverse range of habitats for marine life.

4. Blue Holes: Andros Island is famous for its blue holes, underwater sinkholes that are home to unique ecosystems and geological formations. Many of these blue holes are connected to the barrier reef.

5. Sponge Capital of the World: Andros Island is often referred to as the "Sponge Capital of the World," due to the abundance of sponges found in the reef's waters.

6. Important Fishery: The Andros Barrier Reef plays a vital role in the local economy, supporting a thriving fishing industry.

7. Tourist Destination: The reef attracts divers and snorkelers from around the world, eager to explore its vibrant underwater world.

8. Threatened Ecosystem: The Andros Barrier Reef faces threats from climate change, pollution, and overfishing, making conservation efforts crucial for its survival.

9. Protected Areas: Portions of the reef are protected within the Andros West Side National Park and the North Marine Park, helping to safeguard its unique biodiversity.

10. Research and Conservation: Ongoing research and conservation efforts are focused on understanding and protecting the Andros Barrier Reef, ensuring its preservation for future generations.

Florida Reef Tract (United States)

1. Only Barrier Reef in Continental U.S.: The Florida Reef Tract is the only living coral barrier reef in the continental United States, stretching approximately 360 linear miles from Dry Tortugas National Park to the St. Lucie Inlet.

2. Diverse Ecosystem: It supports over 6,000 species of plants and animals, including more than 40 species of stony corals, 500 species of fish, and hundreds of species of invertebrates.

3. Economic Importance: The reef generates billions of dollars annually for Florida's economy through tourism, fishing, and recreation, supporting over 70,000 jobs.

4. Stony Coral Tissue Loss Disease (SCTLD) Outbreak: The reef is currently facing a devastating outbreak of SCTLD, a disease that has impacted over 20 species of coral and is considered one of the most lethal coral diseases ever recorded.

5. Restoration Efforts: Numerous organisations and government agencies are actively working on coral restoration projects, including growing corals in nurseries and outplanting them onto the reef.

6. Climate Change Threat: The reef is threatened by rising sea temperatures, ocean acidification, and sea-level rise, which can cause coral bleaching and other negative impacts.

7. Protected Areas: Portions of the reef are protected within Biscayne National Park and the Florida Keys National Marine Sanctuary, which help to regulate fishing and other activities.

8. Citizen Science: Volunteers play a crucial role in monitoring the reef's health, reporting sightings of diseased corals, and participating in restoration efforts.

9. Educational Outreach: Education and outreach programs aim to raise awareness about the importance of the reef and encourage responsible behaviour among residents and visitors.

10. Iconic Species: The Florida Reef Tract is home to several iconic species, including the endangered elkhorn and staghorn corals, as well as a variety of colourful fish, sea turtles, and marine mammals.

Saya de Malha Bank

1. The Saya de Malha Bank is a submerged atoll structure in the Indian Ocean, situated roughly midway between Madagascar and Seychelles.

2. It is the largest submerged ocean bank in the world, covering an area of approximately 40,808 square kilometres (15,756 square miles).

3. Despite being underwater, Saya de Malha Bank is home to the world's largest seagrass meadow, a vital ecosystem that acts as a significant carbon sink.

4. This massive seagrass meadow plays a crucial role in mitigating climate change by absorbing and storing vast amounts of carbon dioxide.

5. Saya de Malha Bank supports a diverse range of marine life, including various fish species, sharks, rays, and marine mammals like whales and dolphins.

6. The bank is an important breeding ground for humpback whales and blue whales, which migrate to the area to give birth and raise their young.

7. Due to its remote location and submerged nature, Saya de Malha Bank remains one of the least explored marine environments on Earth.

8. The bank is part of the Mascarene Plateau, a geological feature formed by volcanic activity millions of years ago.

9. Saya de Malha Bank is located in international waters, making it a shared resource requiring international cooperation for its conservation and management.

10. Efforts are underway to establish marine protected areas within Saya de Malha Bank to safeguard its unique ecosystem and biodiversity.

Great Chagos Bank

1. The Great Chagos Bank is the largest atoll structure in the world, encompassing an area of 12,642 km².

2. Despite its size, the majority of the Great Chagos Bank lies submerged, with only a few small islands and emergent coral reefs.

3. It is located in the Chagos Archipelago, approximately 500 km south of the Maldives, in the Indian Ocean.

4. The Great Chagos Bank is part of the British Indian Ocean Territory (BIOT), a disputed overseas territory of the United Kingdom.

5. The atoll is renowned for its rich marine biodiversity, including extensive coral reefs, seagrass meadows, and diverse fish populations.

6. It is a designated no-take marine protected area (MPA), providing a refuge for numerous threatened and endangered species.

7. The submerged reefs of the Great Chagos Bank are an important source of food and shelter for various marine organisms, including sharks, turtles, and seabirds.

8. The atoll plays a crucial role in maintaining the ecological balance of the Indian Ocean by supporting interconnected food webs and nutrient cycles.

9. Due to its remoteness and protected status, the Great Chagos Bank remains relatively pristine, with minimal human impact on its ecosystems.

10. The Great Chagos Bank is a subject of ongoing legal and political disputes between the United Kingdom and Mauritius, with the latter claiming sovereignty over the Chagos Archipelago.

Reed Bank

1. Location: Reed Bank, also known as Recto Bank, is a large, completely submerged atoll located in the northeastern part of the Spratly Islands in the South China Sea.

2. Size: It is approximately 8,866 square kilometres (3,423 square miles) in size, making it one of the largest atolls in the region.

3. Rich in resources: Reed Bank is believed to hold significant reserves of oil and natural gas, making it a focal point of interest for various countries in the region.

4. Disputed territory: The ownership of Reed Bank is disputed, with China, the Philippines, Taiwan, and Vietnam all claiming sovereignty over the area.

5. 2019 incident: In June 2019, a Chinese vessel rammed and sank a Filipino fishing boat in Reed Bank, sparking a diplomatic incident and highlighting the tensions in the region.

6. Importance for the Philippines: Reed Bank is considered to be within the Philippines' exclusive economic zone (EEZ) and holds potential for future energy development for the country.

7. Environmental concerns: The potential exploitation of oil and gas resources in Reed Bank raises environmental concerns due to the risk of spills and damage to marine ecosystems.

8. Geopolitical significance: Reed Bank's location and resource potential make it a strategically important area in the South China Sea, with significant implications for regional security and stability.

9. International law: The Permanent Court of Arbitration in The Hague ruled in 2016 that Reed Bank falls within the Philippines' EEZ, but China has refused to recognise this ruling.

10. Future development: The future of Reed Bank remains uncertain, with ongoing disputes over its ownership and the potential for future resource exploration and development.

Apo Reef

1. Apo Reef is the second-largest contiguous coral reef in the world and the largest atoll reef in the Philippines.

2. It is located in the Mindoro Strait, 33 kilometres west of Sablayan, Occidental Mindoro.

3. Apo Reef Natural Park (ARNP) was established in 1996 to protect the reef and its surrounding waters.

4. ARNP covers a total area of 34 square kilometres, including the reef itself and three islands: Apo Island, Apo Menor, and Cayos del Bajo.

5. The reef is home to a rich biodiversity, with over 450 species of corals and 650 species of fish.

6. Apo Reef is a popular destination for scuba diving and snorkeling, with clear waters and diverse marine life.

7. The reef is an important breeding ground for several marine species, including sea turtles and sharks.

8. Apo Reef Natural Park is a UNESCO World Heritage Site nominee, recognised for its outstanding universal value.

9. The reef is threatened by climate change, pollution, and overfishing.

10. Conservation efforts are underway to protect Apo Reef and its fragile ecosystem, including the implementation of sustainable tourism practices and the establishment of marine protected areas.

Micro-plastic & Reefs

1. Microplastics are tiny plastic particles smaller than 5 millimetres in size, originating from larger plastic debris that breaks down or from microbeads found in personal care products.

2. Coral reefs are particularly vulnerable to microplastic pollution due to their complex structures and filter-feeding mechanisms, which can trap and accumulate these particles.

3. Microplastics can cause physical harm to corals by blocking their feeding structures, reducing their ability to capture food and nutrients.

4. Ingesting microplastics can disrupt the corals' digestive processes and cause inflammation, leading to malnutrition and increased susceptibility to disease.

5. Microplastics can also release toxic chemicals into the coral tissue, further compromising their health and resilience.

6. The accumulation of microplastics on coral reefs can alter the microbial communities living on their surfaces, potentially disrupting important symbiotic relationships.

7. Microplastics can act as vectors for harmful pathogens and pollutants, exacerbating the impacts of other environmental stressors on coral reefs.

8. The presence of microplastics in the reef ecosystem can have cascading effects on the entire food web, impacting fish and other organisms that depend on corals for food and shelter.

9. Research has shown that the presence of microplastics can increase the susceptibility of corals to bleaching, a phenomenon where corals expel their symbiotic algae, leading to their death.

10. Reducing plastic pollution is crucial for the health of coral reefs. Implementing measures to reduce plastic waste, improve waste management, and develop sustainable alternatives are essential steps to mitigate the impacts of microplastics on these fragile ecosystems.

Plastic Waste

1. An estimated 8 million metric tons of plastic enter the oceans each year, equivalent to dumping a garbage truck of plastic into the ocean every minute.

2. Plastic pollution is found in all the world's oceans, from the Arctic to the Antarctic, and even in the deepest parts like the Mariana Trench.

3. The majority of plastic waste in the ocean comes from land-based sources, including improper waste disposal, littering, and industrial activities.

4. Plastic debris harms marine life through ingestion, entanglement, and habitat destruction. Animals mistake plastic for food, leading to starvation and death.

5. Over 700 marine species are known to be affected by plastic pollution, including sea turtles, seabirds, fish, and marine mammals.

6. Plastic debris can also transport invasive species and harmful pathogens across oceans, disrupting ecosystems.

7. Plastic waste breaks down into smaller pieces called microplastics, which can enter the food chain and pose potential risks to human health.

8. Ocean currents can concentrate plastic debris into massive garbage patches, such as the Great Pacific Garbage Patch, which covers an area larger than the state of Texas.

9. Cleaning up plastic waste from the ocean is a monumental challenge, as much of it is fragmented and dispersed over vast areas.

10. Reducing plastic consumption, improving waste management, and promoting recycling are crucial steps to addressing the plastic pollution crisis in our oceans.

Equivalent

The 8 million metric tons of plastic waste entering the ocean annually could be equivalent to approximately 3,333,333 cubic meters of concrete.

A standard 500 ml single-use plastic water bottle weighs roughly 9.9 grams. 8 million metric tons is equivalent to 8 trillion grams. Dividing the total weight of plastic waste (8 trillion grams) by the weight of a single bottle (9.9 grams) yields an estimated 808 billion plastic bottles.

Fish and Plastic

1. Fish ingest microplastics: Studies have shown that a wide range of fish species, from small plankton feeders to large predators, ingest microplastics, mistaking them for food.

2. Plastic accumulates in fish tissues: Ingested microplastics can accumulate in the tissues of fish, potentially causing physical harm and transferring harmful chemicals into their bodies.

3. Plastic impacts fish behaviour and physiology: Exposure to microplastics can alter fish behaviour, impair growth, and affect reproduction, with potential consequences for fish populations.

4. Plastic transfers through the food chain: Microplastics can transfer from smaller fish to larger predators through the food chain, accumulating in higher concentrations at each level.

5. Seafood safety concerns: The presence of microplastics in fish raises concerns about the safety of seafood for human consumption, although the full health impacts are still being investigated.

6. Plastic pollution hotspots: Fish in areas with high levels of plastic pollution, such as coastal regions and ocean gyres, are at greater risk of ingesting microplastics.

7. Plastic impacts fish larvae and juveniles: Early life stages of fish are particularly vulnerable to microplastic exposure, potentially affecting their development and survival.

8. Plastic interacts with other pollutants: Microplastics can act as carriers for other pollutants, such as heavy metals and persistent organic pollutants, increasing their toxicity to fish.

9. Plastic pollution affects fisheries: The impact of plastic on fish populations can have economic consequences for fisheries, affecting the livelihoods of fishing communities.

10. Research and solutions: Ongoing research is investigating the full extent of the impacts of plastic on fish, while efforts to reduce plastic pollution and develop sustainable fishing practices are crucial for protecting marine ecosystems and ensuring the health of fish populations.

Volcanoes

1. Abundance: Underwater volcanoes are estimated to be far more numerous than terrestrial volcanoes, with potentially millions existing beneath the ocean's surface.

2. Formation: They form along mid-ocean ridges, where tectonic plates diverge, and at hotspots, where magma rises from deep within the Earth.

3. Eruptions: Underwater eruptions can be explosive or effusive, releasing lava, ash, and gases into the water.

4. Hydrothermal Vents: These unique ecosystems form around underwater volcanoes, where hot, mineral-rich water supports diverse life forms, including tube worms, giant clams, and chemosynthetic bacteria.

5. Volcanic Islands: Over time, repeated eruptions from underwater volcanoes can lead to the formation of volcanic islands, such as Hawaii and Iceland.

6. Tsunamis: Large underwater eruptions have the potential to trigger tsunamis, powerful waves that can cause widespread destruction.

7. Exploration Challenges: Studying underwater volcanoes is challenging due to the extreme conditions and limited access, requiring specialised equipment and technology.

8. Scientific Importance: Underwater volcanoes offer valuable insights into the Earth's internal processes, the formation of new crust, and the origins of life on our planet.

9. Resources: Some underwater volcanoes host deposits of valuable minerals, such as copper, zinc, and gold, which could potentially be mined in the future.

10. Monitoring and Research: Scientists continue to monitor and study underwater volcanoes to better understand their behaviour, assess potential hazards, and explore their unique ecosystems.

Eruptions

1. Frequency: Underwater eruptions are estimated to be far more common than eruptions on land, occurring almost continuously along the vast network of mid-ocean ridges.

2. Types: Underwater eruptions can be explosive, producing ash plumes and pyroclastic flows, or effusive, releasing lava flows that create new seafloor.

3. Depth Influence: The depth of the eruption greatly influences its characteristics. Shallow eruptions can produce steam explosions and release volcanic gases into the atmosphere, while deeper eruptions are often quieter and generate lava flows.

4. Hydrothermal Vents: Underwater eruptions create hydrothermal vents, where hot, mineral-rich fluids gush from the seafloor, supporting unique ecosystems that thrive in extreme conditions.

5. Seafloor Spreading: Underwater eruptions are the primary mechanism for seafloor spreading, where new oceanic crust is formed at mid-ocean ridges, contributing to plate tectonics.

6. Detection Challenges: Detecting underwater eruptions can be difficult due to their remote locations and the vastness of the oceans. However, scientists use hydrophones, seismometers, and other instruments to monitor volcanic activity.

7. Environmental Impacts: Underwater eruptions can release large amounts of gases, including carbon dioxide and sulphur dioxide, which can affect ocean chemistry and potentially influence climate.

8. Pumice Rafts: Explosive underwater eruptions can create massive pumice rafts, floating masses of volcanic rock that can travel long distances and impact marine ecosystems.

9. Potential Hazards: While most underwater eruptions pose little direct threat to humans, large eruptions in shallow waters can generate tsunamis, posing a risk to coastal communities.

10. Research: Scientists continue to study underwater eruptions to better understand their processes, impacts, and potential hazards, contributing to our knowledge of Earth's dynamic systems.

Fish with Antifreeze

1. Natural Antifreeze Proteins: Antarctic icefish produce special glycoproteins that act as antifreeze, preventing ice crystals from forming in their blood and tissues.

2. Survival in Subzero Temperatures: These fish thrive in the frigid waters of the Southern Ocean, where temperatures can drop below the freezing point of freshwater.

3. Lack of Red Blood Cells: Unlike most vertebrates, icefish lack haemoglobin and red blood cells, giving their blood a transparent or whitish appearance.

4. Increased Oxygen Absorption: The absence of red blood cells allows icefish to absorb oxygen directly from the water through their skin and gills.

5. Thriving in Oxygen-Rich Waters: The cold, oxygen-rich waters of Antarctica are ideal for icefish, as they require high oxygen levels due to their unique physiology.

6. Diverse Species: There are several species of icefish, each with unique adaptations to their specific environments.

7. Vulnerable to Climate Change: As ocean temperatures rise due to climate change, icefish face a significant threat, as their specialised adaptations may not be sufficient to cope with warmer waters.

8. Important Research Subjects: Icefish are valuable research subjects for scientists studying adaptations to extreme environments, oxygen transport, and the effects of climate change on marine life.

9. Conservation Efforts: Due to their vulnerability, conservation efforts are underway to protect icefish populations and their unique habitats.

10. Unique Blood Circulation: Icefish have a larger heart and a higher blood volume compared to other fish, which helps them compensate for the lack of haemoglobin and efficiently transport oxygen throughout their bodies.

Fish with no eyes "FSH"

1. Blind Cavefish: Several species of cavefish have evolved to live in complete darkness and have lost their eyes over generations.

2. Mexican Tetra: The Mexican tetra, also known as the blind cavefish, is a popular aquarium fish that naturally lacks eyes.

3. Adaptation to Darkness: Eyeless fish have adapted to their lightless environments by developing heightened senses of smell, taste, and touch to navigate and find food.

4. Lateral Line System: They rely heavily on their lateral line system, a sensory organ that detects vibrations and pressure changes in the water, to perceive their surroundings.

5. Energy Conservation: The absence of eyes allows eyeless fish to conserve energy, as maintaining vision requires significant resources.

6. Diverse Habitats: Eyeless fish are found in various habitats, including caves, underground rivers, and deep-sea environments where light is scarce or absent.

7. Genetic Mutations: The loss of eyes in these fish is attributed to genetic mutations that occur over time due to the lack of selective pressure to maintain vision.

8. Evolutionary Advantage: In their dark environments, the absence of eyes is not a disadvantage but rather an evolutionary advantage, as it reduces unnecessary energy expenditure.

9. Cavefish Research: Scientists study eyeless fish to understand evolutionary processes, sensory adaptation, and the genetic basis of vision loss.

10. Conservation Concerns: Some eyeless fish species are threatened by habitat destruction and pollution, highlighting the importance of conservation efforts to protect these unique creatures.

Sea Currents

1. Global Circulation: Sea currents play a crucial role in global climate regulation by redistributing heat from the equator towards the poles.

2. Types: There are two main types of currents: surface currents, driven by wind, and deep ocean currents, driven by differences in temperature and salinity.

3. Major Currents: Some of the most well-known currents include the Gulf Stream, the Kuroshio Current, the California Current, and the Antarctic Circumpolar Current.

4. Influence on Weather: Currents influence weather patterns by carrying warm or cold water and moisture, impacting coastal temperatures and rainfall.

5. Marine Life: Currents transport nutrients and plankton, supporting diverse marine ecosystems and influencing the distribution of marine species.

6. Navigation: Mariners have used knowledge of currents for centuries to navigate the seas efficiently and safely.

7. Energy Potential: Harnessing the energy of ocean currents is a developing field of renewable energy research.

8. Climate Change Impact: Climate change is altering ocean currents, with potential consequences for weather patterns, marine ecosystems, and coastal communities.

9. Upwelling and Downwelling: These vertical currents bring nutrient-rich deep water to the surface, fueling plankton blooms and supporting productive fisheries.

10. Research and Monitoring: Scientists use buoys, satellites, and other technologies to study and monitor ocean currents to better understand their role in the Earth's climate system.

Microorganisms

1. Abundance: Microorganisms make up the vast majority of life in the ocean, with trillions of them inhabiting every drop of seawater.

2. Diversity: The ocean's microbial communities are incredibly diverse, comprising bacteria, archaea, viruses, fungi, and protists.

3. Oxygen Production: Marine microorganisms, particularly phytoplankton, are responsible for producing roughly 50% of the oxygen in the Earth's atmosphere.

4. Base of the Food Web: Microorganisms form the foundation of the marine food web, serving as the primary food source for many larger organisms, including zooplankton and fish.

5. Nutrient Cycling: Microorganisms play a crucial role in nutrient cycling in the ocean, breaking down organic matter and releasing nutrients back into the ecosystem.

6. Climate Regulation: Marine microorganisms influence the Earth's climate by absorbing carbon dioxide from the atmosphere and storing it in the ocean depths.

7. Bioluminescence: Some marine microorganisms, such as dinoflagellates, are bioluminescent, producing light through chemical reactions.

8. Symbiotic Relationships: Many marine microorganisms form symbiotic relationships with other organisms, such as corals and sponges, providing them with essential nutrients and other benefits.

9. Disease and Health: Some marine microorganisms can cause diseases in marine life and humans, while others play important roles in maintaining the health of marine ecosystems.

10. Unexplored Diversity: Despite their importance, the vast majority of marine microorganisms remain undiscovered and poorly understood, representing a vast frontier for scientific exploration.

Bioluminescence

1. Widespread Phenomenon: Bioluminescence is surprisingly common in the ocean, with an estimated 90% of deep-sea creatures possessing this ability.

2. Chemical Reaction: Bioluminescence is produced through a chemical reaction involving a light-emitting molecule called luciferin and an enzyme called luciferase.

3. Variety of Purposes: Marine organisms use bioluminescence for various purposes, including attracting prey, communication, camouflage, and defence against predators.

4. Different Colours: Bioluminescence in the ocean comes in various colours, including blue, green, yellow, and even red.

5. Deep-Sea Light Show: The deep ocean is a mesmerising light show of bioluminescent creatures, with flashing lights, glowing tentacles, and shimmering trails.

6. Dinoflagellates: These tiny plankton are responsible for the sparkling displays of bioluminescence often seen in ocean waves at night.

7. Anglerfish: This deep-sea predator uses a bioluminescent lure to attract unsuspecting prey.

8. Vampire Squid: This cephalopod can eject a cloud of bioluminescent mucus to confuse predators and escape.

9. Comb Jellies: These gelatinous creatures create mesmerising displays of bioluminescent light as they move through the water.

10. Research and Applications: Scientists are studying bioluminescence to develop new technologies, such as medical imaging tools and environmental sensors.

Strangest named Sea Dwellers

1. Red-Lipped Batfish: This fish has bright red lips that resemble lipstick, along with modified fins it uses to "walk" along the ocean floor.

2. Pink See-Through Fantasia: This deep-sea cucumber has a translucent body that reveals its internal organs, giving it a surreal and ethereal appearance.

3. Stargazer Fish: This ambush predator buries itself in the sand with only its eyes and mouth protruding, waiting to ambush unsuspecting prey.

4. Yeti Crab: This deep-sea crustacean is covered in hair-like bristles, giving it a fuzzy and somewhat disturbing look.

5. Whitemargin Stargazer: This fish has a face only a mother could love, with a large, upturned mouth filled with sharp teeth and a body covered in venomous spines.

6. Sea Angel: This tiny, translucent sea slug has wing-like appendages and resembles a miniature angel floating through the water.

7. Sea Spider: These eight-legged creatures are not true spiders but are a unique group of arthropods with long, spindly legs and a small body.

8. Blob Sculpin: This fish has a large head and a drooping mouth, giving it a perpetually sad and grumpy appearance.

9. Coffinfish: This deep-sea fish has a bioluminescent lure on its head to attract prey and can inflate its body to deter predators.

10. Sarcastic Fringehead: This fish gets its name from its aggressive territorial behaviour and large, fanged mouth, which it displays in a dramatic, almost sarcastic, fashion.

The Twilight Zone

1. Depth and Light: The twilight zone extends from about 200 to 1,000 meters (656 to 3,280 feet) below the ocean's surface. Sunlight diminishes rapidly at these depths, creating a dim, twilight environment.

2. Abundant Life: Despite the low light levels, the twilight zone teems with life. It is estimated to contain more fish biomass than any other part of the ocean.

3. Vertical Migration: Many twilight zone creatures undergo daily vertical migrations, rising to the surface at night to feed and descending to the depths during the day to avoid predators.

4. Bioluminescence: Many organisms in the twilight zone are bioluminescent, meaning they can produce their own light. This light is used for communication, attracting prey, and camouflage.

5. Mysterious Creatures: The twilight zone is home to many bizarre and fascinating creatures, including lanternfish, vampire squid, and comb jellies.

6. Carbon Cycling: The twilight zone plays a crucial role in the ocean's carbon cycle, as organisms transport carbon from the surface to the depths through their daily migrations and sinking carcasses.

7. Unexplored Territory: Despite its importance, the twilight zone remains largely unexplored due to the challenges of accessing and studying this deep-sea environment.

8. Technological Advances: Recent advances in submersibles and remotely operated vehicles (ROVs) are allowing scientists to explore the twilight zone in greater detail.

9. Potential Resources: The twilight zone may contain valuable resources, such as fish stocks and minerals, but their exploitation raises environmental concerns.

10. Climate Change Impacts: Climate change is likely to affect the twilight zone, potentially disrupting food webs, altering migration patterns, and impacting the ocean's carbon cycle.

Most Diverse Ocean

1. The Ring of Fire: The Pacific Ocean is surrounded by the "Ring of Fire," a zone of intense volcanic and earthquake activity. This geological activity contributes to the creation of new habitats and the diversity of life in the Pacific.

2. Coral Triangle: The Pacific Ocean encompasses the western part of the Coral Triangle, the most bio diverse marine region on Earth. It boasts the highest diversity of coral reef fish species, with over 2,000 species recorded.

3. Deep-Sea Trenches: The Pacific is home to the deepest part of the ocean, the Mariana Trench, reaching a depth of over 36,000 feet (11,000 meters). This extreme environment harbours unique and bizarre deep-sea creatures.

4. Migratory Megafauna: The vast expanse of the Pacific provides essential migratory routes for numerous large marine animals, including whales, sharks, sea turtles, and seabirds.

5. Unique Ecosystems: The Pacific Ocean encompasses a variety of unique ecosystems, from lush coral reefs to hydrothermal vents teeming with life forms that rely on chemosynthesis rather than sunlight for energy.

6. Endemic Species: The Pacific boasts a high number of endemic species, meaning they are found nowhere else on Earth. This includes species like the Hawaiian monk seal and the Galapagos penguin.

7. Marine Mammal Diversity: The Pacific Ocean is home to a diverse array of marine mammals, including several species of whales, dolphins, seals, and sea lions.

8. Fish Abundance: The Pacific supports the largest fisheries in the world, with a wide variety of fish species contributing to global food security.

9. Seabird Colonies: Numerous islands and coastal areas in the Pacific provide nesting grounds for vast colonies of seabirds, making it an important region for bird conservation.

10. Research and Exploration: The Pacific Ocean remains a frontier for scientific exploration, with new species and ecosystems still being discovered, revealing the immense complexity and richness of this vast ocean.

How Much Water

1. Staggering Volume: The Earth's oceans hold approximately 1.335 billion cubic kilometres (321 million cubic miles) of water, a volume that's difficult to comprehend.

2. Percentage of Earth's Water: Oceans account for about 96.5% of all the water on Earth. The remaining 3.5% is found in freshwater sources like lakes, rivers, ice caps, and groundwater.

3. Distribution: The Pacific Ocean is the largest and deepest, holding more than half of the Earth's seawater. The Atlantic Ocean is the second largest, followed by the Indian, Southern, and Arctic Oceans.

4. Constant Movement: The water in the oceans is constantly in motion, driven by currents, tides, and winds. This movement plays a crucial role in distributing heat, nutrients, and marine life around the planet.

5. Depth: The average depth of the ocean is about 2.3 miles (3.7 kilometres), but some areas, like the Mariana Trench, reach depths of over 7 miles (11 kilometres).

6. Salinity: Seawater is salty due to the presence of dissolved minerals, primarily sodium chloride (table salt). The average salinity of seawater is about 3.5%, but it can vary depending on location and factors like evaporation and freshwater input.

7. Temperature: The temperature of seawater varies widely depending on location, depth, and season. Surface water temperatures can range from below freezing in polar regions to over 90°F (32°C) in tropical areas.

8. Pressure: Water pressure increases with depth, reaching immense levels in the deep ocean. At the bottom of the Mariana Trench, the pressure is over 1,000 times greater than at the surface.

9. Life Support: The oceans are home to a vast array of marine life, from microscopic plankton to giant whales. This biodiversity is supported by the ocean's complex physical and chemical properties.

10. Climate Regulation: The oceans play a crucial role in regulating the Earth's climate by absorbing heat, storing carbon dioxide, and influencing weather patterns.

How Salty

1. Immense Quantity: If you extracted all the salt from the oceans and spread it evenly over the Earth's land surface, it would create a layer about 500 feet (166 meters) thick.

2. Source of Salt: The salt in the ocean comes primarily from rocks on land. Rainwater dissolves minerals from rocks, and these dissolved minerals are carried by rivers to the ocean.

3. Salinity Measurement: Salinity is measured in parts per thousand (ppt). The average salinity of seawater is about 35 ppt, meaning that 3.5% of the weight of seawater comes from dissolved salts.

4. Variations in Salinity: Salinity varies across different parts of the ocean. It's generally lower near the equator and poles due to higher rainfall and melting ice, and higher in subtropical regions due to higher evaporation rates.

5. Most Abundant Salts: The two most common ions in seawater are chloride and sodium, which together make up about 85% of all dissolved ions in the ocean.

6. Other Salts: Seawater also contains smaller amounts of magnesium, sulfate, calcium, potassium, and other trace elements.

7. Constant Input: The ocean's salt content is not static. Rivers and hydrothermal vents continuously add new minerals to the ocean, while biological processes and chemical reactions remove some salts.

8. Salt Balance: Despite the constant input and removal of salts, the overall salinity of the ocean remains relatively stable over long periods.

9. Importance for Life: The salt in the ocean plays a crucial role in marine life. It affects the density of seawater, influences ocean currents, and provides essential minerals for marine organisms.

10. Human Impact: Human activities, such as pollution and climate change, can alter the ocean's salinity patterns, potentially affecting marine ecosystems and the services they provide.

Why Salt

1. Erosion and Weathering of Rocks: The primary source of salt in the oceans is the gradual erosion and weathering of rocks on land. Rainwater, slightly acidic from atmospheric carbon dioxide, dissolves minerals from rocks, carrying them to rivers and eventually the ocean.

2. Hydrothermal Vents: Another source of salt is hydrothermal vents on the ocean floor. These vents release superheated water containing dissolved minerals from Earth's interior.

3. Volcanic Eruptions: Underwater volcanic eruptions also contribute to the salt content of the oceans by directly releasing minerals into the water.

4. River Runoff: Rivers carry dissolved salts from land to the ocean. While river water is not as salty as seawater, the continuous influx over millions of years contributes significantly to ocean salinity.

5. Evaporation and Precipitation: Evaporation removes water molecules from the ocean surface, leaving the salt behind. This process increases the salinity of the remaining water. Precipitation, on the other hand, dilutes the salt concentration.

6. Ocean Circulation: Ocean currents distribute salt throughout the world's oceans, helping to maintain a relatively constant average salinity.

7. Biological Processes: Some marine organisms, such as shellfish and corals, extract calcium carbonate from seawater to build their shells and skeletons. This process removes some salts from the water.

8. Salt Deposits: In some areas with high evaporation rates, salt can accumulate and form vast salt deposits on the seafloor or along coastlines.

9. Importance for Life: The salt in the ocean is essential for many forms of marine life, affecting water density, ocean currents, and providing essential minerals for organisms.

10. Dynamic Equilibrium: The ocean's salt content is not static but is maintained in a dynamic equilibrium through a complex interplay of natural processes that add and remove salt over time.

History

1. Early Formation: The oceans are believed to have formed over 4 billion years ago, primarily from water vapor released by volcanic activity and icy comets that collided with Earth.

2. Initial Composition: The early oceans were likely much more acidic and hotter than today's oceans due to the presence of dissolved volcanic gases and the lack of oxygen.

3. Oxygenation: The rise of photosynthetic organisms, such as cyanobacteria, led to the Great Oxygenation Event around 2.4 billion years ago. This drastically changed the ocean's chemistry and paved the way for more complex life forms.

4. Supercontinent Cycle: The Earth's continents have gone through cycles of joining together (forming supercontinents) and breaking apart. These cycles have significantly influenced ocean currents, temperatures, and the distribution of marine life.

5. Sea Level Fluctuations: Throughout Earth's history, sea levels have risen and fallen dramatically due to factors like glacial cycles, tectonic activity, and changes in the Earth's orbit.

6. Mass Extinctions: The oceans have witnessed several mass extinction events, including the Permian-Triassic extinction, which wiped out about 96% of marine species.

7. Evolution of Marine Life: The oceans have been a cradle of evolution, giving rise to a vast array of diverse marine life forms over billions of years.

8. Ancient Seaways: In the past, vast seaways connected continents that are now separated, allowing for the migration and dispersal of marine organisms.

9. Fossil Record: The fossil record of marine organisms provides valuable insights into the evolution of life in the oceans and the changing conditions of the ancient seas.

10. Human Impacts: In recent centuries, human activities such as pollution, overfishing, and climate change have begun to significantly impact the oceans, threatening marine biodiversity and ecosystem health.

Prehistoric

1. Early Oceans: The first oceans on Earth were likely formed by volcanic outgassing and icy comets impacting the planet, gradually accumulating water over millions of years.

2. Acidic Waters: Early oceans were probably highly acidic due to dissolved volcanic gases, such as carbon dioxide and sulfur dioxide. These conditions would have been hostile to most modern life forms.

3. Oxygen Revolution: The rise of photosynthetic organisms, like cyanobacteria, led to the Great Oxygenation Event around 2.4 billion years ago. This drastically changed the ocean's chemistry, making it more hospitable to complex life.

4. Panthalassa: During the late Paleozoic and early Mesozoic eras, the supercontinent Pangaea was surrounded by a single vast ocean called Panthalassa.

5. Tethys Ocean: The Tethys Ocean existed between the ancient continents of Gondwana and Laurasia, playing a crucial role in the evolution and distribution of marine life.

6. Giant Marine Reptiles: Prehistoric oceans were home to a variety of now-extinct marine reptiles, including plesiosaurs, ichthyosaurs, and mosasaurs.

7. Megalodon: This giant prehistoric shark, Carcharocles megalodon, was the largest shark to have ever lived, reaching lengths of up to 60 feet (18 meters).

8. Ammonites: These extinct cephalopods with coiled shells were abundant in prehistoric oceans and are now valuable fossils for dating rock layers.

9. Sea Level Changes: Sea levels have fluctuated dramatically throughout Earth's history due to glacial cycles, tectonic activity, and other factors.

10. Fossil Discoveries: The study of marine fossils has revealed much about prehistoric oceans, including the evolution of marine life, past climates, and changes in ocean chemistry over time.

Monsters

1. Diverse Group: Prehistoric marine reptiles were a diverse group, including ichthyosaurs (fish-like), plesiosaurs (long-necked), mosasaurs (lizard-like), and placodonts (armored shell-like).

2. Dominated the Seas: For over 150 million years, these reptiles were the dominant predators of the oceans, filling ecological niches similar to modern whales, dolphins, and sharks.

3. Size Range: Prehistoric marine reptiles varied greatly in size, from the small, dolphin-like ichthyosaurs to the massive, bus-sized mosasaurs like Mosasaurus and Tylosaurus.

4. Adaptations for Aquatic Life: These reptiles developed various adaptations for life in the water, including streamlined bodies, flippers, and powerful tails for efficient swimming. Some even evolved the ability to give birth to live young underwater.

5. Global Distribution: Fossils of marine reptiles have been found on every continent, indicating their widespread presence in ancient oceans.

6. Apex Predators: Many marine reptiles were apex predators, preying on fish, squid, other marine reptiles, and even dinosaurs that ventured too close to the water.

7. Extinction: Most marine reptiles went extinct at the end of the Cretaceous period, along with the dinosaurs, likely due to a combination of factors, including asteroid impact, volcanic activity, and climate change.

8. Fossil Discoveries: Fossil discoveries have revealed much about the anatomy, behavior, and evolutionary history of these fascinating creatures. Some of the most complete and well-preserved specimens have been found in locations like the Smoky Hill Chalk of Kansas and the Jurassic Coast of England.

9. Modern Relatives: While most marine reptiles are extinct, some modern reptiles, such as sea turtles and sea snakes, are distant relatives of these ancient creatures.

10. Iconic Examples: Some of the most well-known and iconic prehistoric marine reptiles include the dolphin-like Ichthyosaurus, the long-necked Elasmosaurus, the ferocious Mosasaurus, and the giant sea turtle Archelon.

Jurassic Coasts

1. World Heritage Site: The Jurassic Coast is England's only natural UNESCO World Heritage Site, recognised for its geological significance and fossil record.

2. 185 Million Years of History: The coastline spans a remarkable 185 million years of geological history, showcasing rock formations from the Triassic, Jurassic, and Cretaceous periods.

3. Fossil Haven: The Jurassic Coast is a treasure trove of fossils, offering a unique glimpse into prehistoric life. Fossils of marine reptiles, dinosaurs, ammonites, and other ancient creatures have been discovered along its shores.

4. Dramatic Cliffs and Landforms: The coastline features stunning cliffs, arches, stacks, and other geological formations, shaped by millions of years of erosion and tectonic activity.

5. "Walk Through Time": A walk along the Jurassic Coast is like a journey through time, with the oldest rocks found in the west and the youngest in the east.

6. Diverse Habitats: The Jurassic Coast supports a variety of habitats, from rocky shores and sandy beaches to coastal grasslands and heathlands, providing a home for numerous plant and animal species.

7. Geological Research Hub: The Jurassic Coast is a major site for geological research, attracting scientists from around the world to study its unique rock formations and fossil record.

8. Popular Tourist Destination: The Jurassic Coast's scenic beauty and rich fossil heritage attract millions of visitors each year, contributing significantly to the local economy.

9. Conservation Efforts: Conservation organisations and local communities work together to protect the Jurassic Coast's unique geological and ecological heritage for future generations.

10. Educational Resource: The Jurassic Coast serves as an invaluable educational resource, providing opportunities for learning about Earth's history, geology, and the evolution of life.

The Most Famous

1. Largest Predator: Megalodon was the largest known predatory fish, estimated to reach lengths of up to 60 feet (18 meters) or more.

2. Powerful Bite: Its massive jaws were lined with serrated teeth up to 7 inches (18 centimetres) long, capable of crushing bones and delivering a powerful bite force.

3. Apex Predator: Megalodon was an apex predator, meaning it sat at the top of the food chain and had no natural predators.

4. Global Distribution: Megalodon fossils have been found on every continent except Antarctica, indicating its wide distribution in ancient oceans.

5. Extinction: Megalodon went extinct around 3.6 million years ago, likely due to a combination of factors, including climate change, changes in prey availability, and competition from other predators.

6. Fossil Evidence: Megalodon fossils primarily consist of teeth and vertebrae, as its skeleton was made of cartilage, which doesn't fossilise well.

7. Pop Culture Icon: Megalodon has become a popular icon in movies, books, and documentaries, often portrayed as a monstrous and terrifying creature.

8. Scientific Significance: Studying Megalodon fossils provides valuable insights into the evolution of sharks, ancient marine ecosystems, and the impacts of climate change on marine life.

9. Ongoing Research: Scientists continue to study Megalodon fossils and the environments in which they lived to better understand this fascinating creature and its place in Earth's history.

10. Mystery and Intrigue: Despite its fame, much about Megalodon remains a mystery, such as its exact behaviour, social structure, and the reasons for its extinction. This air of mystery adds to its allure and keeps scientists and the public fascinated by this ancient ocean giant.

What we should learn

1. The Ocean's Importance to Life: The ocean produces over half of the world's oxygen and absorbs a significant amount of carbon dioxide, playing a vital role in regulating the Earth's climate and supporting countless ecosystems.

2. Biodiversity Hotspot: The ocean is home to a vast array of life, from microscopic plankton to giant whales. Understanding this biodiversity is crucial for appreciating the interconnectedness of life on Earth and for conservation efforts.

3. Threat of Pollution: Human activities, such as plastic pollution and chemical runoff, are severely impacting marine life and ecosystems. Learning about these threats can inspire action to reduce our environmental footprint.

4. Overfishing Crisis: Unsustainable fishing practices are depleting fish stocks and disrupting marine food webs. Understanding the consequences of overfishing can lead to more responsible seafood consumption and support for sustainable fisheries management.

5. Climate Change Impact: Rising sea levels, ocean acidification, and coral bleaching are just a few of the ways climate change is affecting the ocean. Learning about these impacts can motivate us to reduce greenhouse gas emissions and support climate action.

6. Ocean Exploration: Vast areas of the ocean remain unexplored, holding countless mysteries and potential discoveries. Learning about ocean exploration can spark curiosity and inspire the next generation of scientists and explorers.

7. Cultural Significance: The ocean has played a central role in human history, shaping cultures, economies, and livelihoods. Learning about the cultural significance of the ocean can deepen our appreciation for its role in our lives.

8. Ocean Conservation: Marine protected areas, sustainable fishing practices, and pollution reduction efforts are crucial for the health of the ocean. Understanding these conservation initiatives can empower us to support and participate in them.

9. The Ocean's Beauty and Wonder: The ocean is a source of awe and inspiration, with its vastness, diverse ecosystems, and stunning creatures. Taking the time to appreciate its beauty can foster a deeper connection with nature.

10. Our Responsibility: As inhabitants of this planet, we all have a responsibility to protect the ocean and its resources. Learning about the ocean can help us make informed choices and take actions to ensure its health for future generations.

Summary

In our exploration of the ocean's wonders, we've delved into a wide array of fascinating topics:

We uncovered surprising facts about sea crabs, from their ancient origins to their unique communication methods and diverse habitats.

We learned about the astonishing speed of the fastest fish in the sea, the sailfish, and the intriguing adaptations that allow them to thrive.

We examined the vibrant biodiversity of the Pacific Ocean, home to the world's largest coral reef systems and a multitude of unique creatures.

We explored the mysterious "Twilight Zone," a dimly lit region teeming with life and playing a crucial role in the ocean's carbon cycle.

We examined the vital importance of microscopic organisms in maintaining the ocean's health and productivity.

We learned about the captivating phenomenon of bioluminescence, a magical light show produced by various marine creatures.

We encountered some of the strangest and most uniquely named inhabitants of the deep, showcasing the ocean's incredible diversity.

We uncovered lesser-known facts about the ocean's vastness, its salt content, and the crucial role it plays in regulating Earth's climate.

We explored the history of the oceans, from their ancient origins to the impact of human activities on their delicate ecosystems.

We learned about the importance of conserving the ocean and its resources, recognising our responsibility to protect this vital part of our planet.

The ocean is a world of endless wonder, a source of inspiration, and a crucial component of our planet's health. By understanding and appreciating its complexities, we can work together to ensure its preservation for future generations.